One Small
Barking Dog

Ed Gungor

One Small Barking Dog

How to Live a Life That's Hard to Ignore

HOWARD BOOKS
A DIVISION OF SIMON & SCHUSTER, INC.

New York   Nashville   London   Toronto   Sydney

Published by Howard Books, a division of Simon & Schuster, Inc.
1230 Avenue of the Americas, New York, NY 10020
www.howardpublishing.com

Library of Congress Cataloging-in-Publication Data

Gungor, Ed.
   One small barking dog : how to live a life that's hard to ignore / Ed Gungor.
      p.   cm.
   Includes bibliographical references
   1. Christian life. I. Title.
   BV4501.3.G858 2010
   248.4—dc22   2009039654

ISBN 978-1-4767-8644-5

10   9   8   7   6   5   4   3   2   1

HOWARD and colophon are registered trademarks of Simon & Schuster, Inc.

Manufactured in the United States of America

For information regarding special discounts for bulk purchases,
please contact: Simon & Schuster Special Sales at 1-866-506-1949
or business@simonandschuster.com.

The Simon & Schuster Speakers Bureau can bring authors to your live event.
For more information or to book an event, contact the Simon & Schuster Speakers
Bureau at 1-866-248-3049 or visit our website at www.simonspeakers.com.

Edited by Between the Lines
Interior design by Davina Mock-Maniscalco

This book is dedicated to Gail Marie Gungor—
the girl of my dreams, my best friend, and lover. We are
now in our fourth decade together and she not only is
the key witness to all the good and bad the gift of life has
afforded us, she still makes my liver quiver. There is no one
I'd rather grow old with.

Contents

First Thoughts

M Y DOG'S NAME IS FRANK. He is a little white-haired terrier. He may be small, but he lives large in the Gungor family. He thinks he's one of us and believes his is the role of protector. If you came to my door right now and we were trying to talk, Frank would be a force with which we'd have to reckon. He'd be freaking out that a "stranger" is at the door. And his bark is unnerving. He doesn't have the high-pitched *arf-arf-arf* of tiny dogs— it's more of a midtoned *rarf, rarf, rarf!* And he would just keep on barking until I yelled, "QUIET! Go to your kennel!" at least a couple of times. Then he'd reluctantly shut it down and stroll toward his kennel, stopping every few feet to look back, grumbling under his breath.

It's not that Frank is overpowering. Nor does he elicit fear. He certainly doesn't project any kind of authority. He's just a little dog. But you can't ignore him either—he's too *there*. And he makes his thereness known.

Small dogs are like that. They may not run the world, but you can't tune them out—especially when they're speaking. I've learned some great life lessons from Frank. In a way, I think God wants people to be more like the small dogs. It's true that God made "big dogs" too—the good-looking, excessively talented power people. But I don't think they do the most to change the world.

Maybe you feel like one of the small dogs, but if your life consistently carries the tone of the eternal, you can't be ignored. I believe that, for the most part, the world gets changed by "small" people. I am small. We smalls may not run the world, but neither can the world tune us out. If it weren't for small dogs, the world might be a much quieter place; but it would be a needier one as well.

Having spoken up for small dogs and having acknowledged my attachment to Frank, let me add that I'm not a dog lover in the general sense. For instance, there's Fluffy, the tiny dog that lives next door. She's not a small dog. She's microscopic—a four-legged, rodent-like creature with an incessant, high-pitched yap. If she tried to live at my house, Fluffy and I would have to discuss adoption options. Neither do I get along with my wife's sister's dog, Bear. He's too big and lumbering. I'll give him credit for settling down a little since the neutering, but our relationship wouldn't have survived his puppy phase. He was a mammoth, uncoordinated black lab who either knocked over or chewed everything. I just can't do high-maintenance dogs.

But Frank has been good for me. Coaching me in the way of the small dog, he has made me a better person—even a better person of faith. I'm a follower of Jesus, and in my attempts to follow him more closely, I've discovered that God speaks to me through all sorts of things—circumstances, relationships, events, weird relatives, and even my dog—to show me what he wants me to learn.

Frank is my current tutor in the art of living the small-dog life. It's true that he has his issues (as do all of us). But all in all, he is a dog that knows who he is and what he wants in life. He's a small dog with a mission.

I've been seeking the way of the small dog for some time now. If you join me, I guarantee we won't be ignored in this world.

Ed Gungor
Tulsa, OK

PART ONE

Small Is
the New Big

> A person's a person, no matter how small.
> DR. SEUSS

F RANK LEADS AN EVERYDAY SMALL dog's life. He's never been on TV; he's never won Best of Show; and there are only a few people in the world who could actually pick him out in a crowd or a photo. He gets up around the same time every day, runs outside to do his business, comes back in to get some chow and water, plays with a few of his squeaky toys, and then settles in for his midmorning nap. That's about as good as it gets on any given day. Oh . . . he has his moments of thrill—the occasional ride in the car with the window down, the surprise visit from a friend with a dog—but for the most part, Frank's life is predictable. And he's cool with that. He seems very comfortable in his own fur.

I, like Frank, have a pretty predictable everyday life. Except for the occasional, "Hey, don't I know you?" from someone unfamiliar, there are only a few people who could actually pick me out in a photo. I got up this morning, spent some time with God, paid my bills, answered e-mails, prayed with a friend who was rushing his young son to the hospital (the boy was dehydrated from a bad bout with the flu), ran a few errands, and did some writing (my job). For the most part, my daily life is . . . well . . . daily. True, I have a bump or two of excitement and opportunity from time to time, but all in all, my life (like Frank's and like most of the rest of us) is lived out in a zone called ordinary.

But I'm not nearly as content in that state as Frank. Truth is, I've always struggled with being everydayish—almost like it's a sign that my life doesn't really matter. I keep thinking that if I mattered, there should be more *ba da bing ba da boom* going on. And I want to matter. Otherwise, what's the point? I certainly don't want to be just another consumer . . . consumerism seems so soul-less. I think most of us want to be more than users; most want to live in a way that makes the world a better place, a safer place, a more beautiful place, a place with less injustice. The billion-dollar question is how. How does one come to matter? And then, if that question can be answered, how do we know when we do matter—how does one measure such things?

In this first part of our journey together, we'll re-think the concept of being small dogs in a big world, and we'll discover why small is such a big idea.

Chapter 1

Rethink Small

AMERICA IS A HERO CULTURE. Prominence rules. Inconspicuous means insignificant. We tend to think only those who stand out are worthy of adulation. So the standout beautiful, standout rich, standout talented, fairy-tale people are the only ones who seem to matter—and they are our idols; our American idols. Somehow, these values tell us that it's only the standout people who have worth. If people don't stick out—if they are average, ordinary—they are cellophane. Nobody notices cellophane.

We live in a world that insists one must be way beyond ordinary to matter. If that is the case, I don't make the cut. I'm a few degrees south of good looking, and I live several miles outside the gated community of the rich, famous, and overtly talented (arguably, I'm living in a van down by the river by comparison). So, what about those of us who belong to the unbeautiful, seemingly unimportant, ordinary crowd? Are we doomed to taking a number and getting in the queue of the "insignificants"—along with the other stingerless drones taking up space in the human hive?

Something in me doesn't want to accept that. Something in me finds the notion of insignificance as scary as suicide. I want to make a mark on this rock, and I think God is the author of that longing. However, I think most of us are mixed up about this whole concept of significance. I think we struggle with the who-am-I-in-the-scheme-of-things question, plus we misjudge whether we matter because consciously (or unconsciously) we have bought into the myth that prominence is the only sign of significance. So if we're not famous or amazing in some way, we feel hopeless.

An Upside-Down Culture

Some time ago I stumbled across a story in a book by Dallas Willard about a military pilot who was practicing some tricky, high-speed maneuvers on a cloudy day.

As she turned the controls to enter a steep ascent, she plowed straight into the ground. Without realizing it, she had been flying upside down.[1] This is a tragic illustration of how our culture is oriented about things we value—we're upside down. And just like that pilot, our pull-up solutions to go higher in life seem to make matters worse, pretty consistently crashing us into the ground.

Nowhere are we more upside down than in our beliefs about what constitutes greatness or how one can influence the lives of others. Jesus Christ never suggested that standing out in some way is how a person makes his or her mark on the world. Jesus constantly made statements like, "The greatest among you will be your servant,"[2] or "The last will be first, and the first will be last."[3] Those statements redefine the pathway to greatness. The belief that prominence is the necessary prerequisite to be able to write one's life large is a belief that flies against the view Jesus espoused.

Yet the belief that one must stand out to truly succeed is held dearly in the West. This is why so many people are willing to do whatever they must to get into the spotlight—like waiting in long lines, willing to do the craziest things, to get on one of the "reality" TV shows. Those shows have become popular precisely because they give the average Joe and Jane hope that even ordinary people can be worshipped and adored. No wonder so many rush to the surgeon-gods to augment, cut down, suck out, pin back, and rearrange their bodies to improve their appearance. If standout beauty is a must, the pain is worth it—no one wants to be cellophane.

On the other hand, what if the whole standout notion is false? What if you don't have to be beautiful, sexy, rich, famous, or standout anything in order to get your due in this world? One could argue that many things that are significant—even critical—don't stand out at all; they are completely inconspicuous. Things like gravity and oxygen are inconspicuous, yet if they were gone, you wouldn't be reading this. Or think about your physical body—your eyes are obviously more prominent than your lungs, but are they more significant? You can live without eyes. Your hands are more standoutish than your liver, but you can't live without a liver. What if it's the inconspicuous things that are the most crucial to our survival?

What if that holds true for the human family as well? What if those of us who appear average are the ones who matter most? Maybe that's why those who are standout amazing and adored are always seeking ways to have a "normal life." Maybe normal is better than folks normally think.

Few people think it's okay to grow up "just" to be

butchers or bakers or candlestick makers—not if one wants to change the world. But what if that's a lie? Don't misunderstand me: I do believe that some folks have been destined by God to do unusual things— things that are glamorous and weighty in the eyes of humanity. But what if such people are the exception rather than the rule? What if the best, most influential life is the everyday kind?

Actor Jimmy Stewart once explained why he believed the movie *It's a Wonderful Life* was, and continues to be, so immensely popular:

> It wasn't the elaborate movie set, however, that made *It's a Wonderful Life* so different; it was the story. The character I played was George Bailey, an ordinary fella who thinks he's never accomplished anything in life. His dreams of becoming a famous architect, of living adventurously, have not been fulfilled. Instead he feels trapped in a humdrum job in a small town. And when faced with a crisis in which he feels he has failed everyone, he breaks under the strain and flees to the bridge. That's when his guardian angel, Clarence, comes down on Christmas Eve to show him what his community would be like without him. The angel takes him

back through his life to show how our ordinary everyday efforts are really big achievements.

Clarence reveals how George Bailey's loyalty to his job at the building-and-loan office has saved families and homes, how his little kindnesses have changed the lives of others and how the ripples of his love will spread through the world, helping make it a better place. . . .

Today, after some 40 years, I've heard the film called "an American cultural phenomenon." Well, maybe so, but it seems to me there is nothing phenomenal about the movie itself. It's simply about an ordinary man who discovers that living each ordinary day honorably, with faith in God and a selfless concern for others, can make for a truly wonderful life.[4]

When we take time to look back on our lives, we discover that the people who impacted our lives the most were not the amazing human luminaries of the world—the gloriously gifted, shockingly beautiful, or imposingly brilliant. Instead, the greatest impact came from our moms and dads, our friends and neighbors—the small dogs. Sure, we've all been thrilled, educated, entertained, and even inspired by the big standout people, but our lives have not been changed by them.

In central Wisconsin, where I grew up, a printing company was owned by the kind, hardworking Heinzen family. I remember walking in one day to place a print order and noticing a plaque that honored the lives of Benjamin and Gerald Heinzen, men of two previous generations, no longer living. The plaque hung conspicuously on the wall of the reception area. In a simple yet profound way, it reflected the family's belief that a life well lived is really what defines greatness. It read: "I have seen my own parents, who never became famous or did 'great' things in the eyes of the world achieve something spectacular. They achieved a life of quiet service to their family and community."

I think the greatest heroes in our world are of the George Bailey/Ben and Jerry Heinzen sort. But in a culture where Tinseltown values rule the day, their ilk seems to be going the way of the dinosaur.

Getting people to buy into the concept of being okay with ordinary is a hard sell. It's so countercultural. And it takes great vision (you have to peer beyond the obvious) and lots of guts. It is obviously more glamorous to make one's way in life as a famous person or to land "big deals" as a successful businessperson than it is to make sure you have time to take your spouse out on dates or to play miniature golf with your kids. But what if most of us were not designed to be famous or to do "great" things in the spotlight before an adoring world? Is it possible that greatness can be most accurately judged when we take a longer view?

In her book *Marriage to a Difficult Man: The Uncommon Union of Jonathan and Sarah Edwards*, Elisabeth D. Dodds shows how a mother's influence can continue to impact the world for generations after she has gone. The book reveals the achievements and contributions of the descendants of Sarah Edwards and her husband, the famous eighteenth-century preacher Jonathan Edwards. From the eleven children and a multitude of grandchildren, great-grandchildren, and subsequent generations, as of 1900 the family had produced thirteen college presidents; sixty-five professors; one hundred lawyers; a dean of a law school; thirty judges; sixty-six physicians; a dean of a medical school; and eighty public-office holders, including three mayors, three governors, three United States senators, a controller of the United States Treasury, and a vice president of the United States.

Chances are Sarah Edwards was unable to foresee all this as she fed, clothed, and invested her love and values in her children. She probably felt she was doing little for the world while mothering them through the daily grind of life—unless she was looking at what she was doing through eyes of vision and faith.

We are much more likely to view the ordinary aspects of life, like raising children, as more of an imposition than a mission, as demonstrated in this story about historian Brooks Adams, great-grandson of John Adams and grandson of John Quincy Adams:

Brooks Adams kept a diary from his boyhood. One special day, when he was eight years old he wrote in his diary: "Went fishing with my Dad, the most glorious day of my life."

Throughout the next 40 years of his life he kept a diary and he never forgot that day he went fishing with his dad and through the diary he makes repeated references commenting on the influence that this day had in his life.

Brooks' father was an important man—he was Charles Francis Adams, the U.S. Ambassador to Great Britain under the Lincoln Administration. Interestingly, he too made a note in his diary about that fishing trip. This is what he wrote: "Went fishing with my son, a day wasted."[5]

Radical Ordinariness

From the Western point of view, being ordinary means we're "just another one of them," which signifies that we are nothing in particular—thus proving we have little value. But something in us silently screams with deadening agony at that notion. This is why each of us, from the smallest child to the oldest adult, wants to be different; outstanding in some way; unique, extraordinary. Even just fifteen minutes of fame that Andy Warhol said everyone in our modern media world would someday have is a welcome insulation against the stigma of being a "nobody."

But here's a provocative thought: it appears that the beachhead for God's spilling his life into the world is the dreaded ordinary. When you study the Bible and the lives of the saints throughout history, it seems "ordinary" is the chosen habitation of the eternal. Consider Jesus. He was born in a manger (certainly not the experience of the rich and famous of his day). He grew up in a small village with a bad reputation ("Nazareth! Can anything good come from there?"[6]) and was raised in the home of a carpenter. Jesus, it turned out, was a blue-collar worker. He did this to be with us, to be one of us—to bring the eternal into the world through the ordinariness of life.

The message Christ-followers refer to as the gospel is more than a ticket to make the cut when we die. The gospel is a call to allow Jesus Christ to heal, empower, and inform our individual human experience. And in the interaction that occurs with the Savior, ordinary people encounter a life that is greater than just human existence—it's a life that has the quality of eternity.

Amazingly, God's life does not destroy ordinary, everyday human life; it actually fulfills and empowers it. Dallas Willard wrote: "The obviously well kept secret of the 'ordinary' is that it is made to be a receptacle of the divine, a place where the life of God flows."[7] According to this view, being small, basic, ordinary, and merely human (with human limitations, blind spots, and all the rest) is absolutely the best thing that ever could have happened to us. That's because our unspectacular traits are the perfect springboards for the divine. It turns out that small is the new big.

What's odd about all this is that when God generates significant influence through our lives, we're often completely unaware of it. The most influential folks in my life were the ones who, without an act or conscious performance, were just being themselves around me. They changed the way I lived, yet most of them never even realized it.

Brother Hamloth, as he liked to be called, was an old farmer who was a deacon in the church I grew up attending. He was a six-foot-four, portly, sixty-something guy who was always jovial and interested in others—even in me as a teenager. One afternoon I went out to see him at his farm in the middle of no-where in central Wisconsin. After giving me the tour, he took me out to the edge of the field next to his dairy barn. He paused for a moment and, with a hint of tears in his eyes, pointed over to a spot in the field of corn five feet high and told me: "I used to stand right over there when I was a kid, and God would meet me. I could feel his smile."

I remember looking wide-eyed to where he was pointing and thinking, *I want to feel God's smile. I want to know God better.* That brief moment changed my life forever. In a sentence, Brother Hamloth communicated to my soul a longing to grow in my faith in a way no sermon had ever done. To this day that story frames my life in a sweet way—yet Brother Hamloth never knew it. He probably thought he was just cellophane.

Surprise, Surprise

A few years back I was in Missouri to teach at a men's retreat. Several hours before heading off to the retreat, I visited a mall. I wandered around, thinking and pray-ing about my sessions more than I was shopping, and entered a Successories store. As I perused the books and plaques, I noticed the salesperson out of the corner of my eye. She faced the wall behind the cash register as she talked on the phone. Immediately I sensed that something was wrong. I'm not much of a spooky, spiritual guy, but every once in a while I feel a strong drawing of the Holy Spirit in everyday situations. This was one of those times. As I took a second glance, I noticed she was crying. When she hung up the phone and was trying to compose herself, I approached her.

"Excuse me, miss," I said softly. "I'm a pastor, and I was over there looking at some of your stuff and minding my own business. But when I looked at you, I felt like God wanted me to come over here and pray for you. Is anything wrong?"

Instantly she broke out in violent, gasping sobs—tears squirting from her eyes. Frankly, I was a bit embarrassed, and I was thankful no one else was in the store. She tried but couldn't talk. She couldn't push past those little hiccupy sobs that young kids get.

"You don't have to say anything," I told her. "Is it okay if I pray for you?"

She nodded gratefully.

"Jesus," I began, "I don't know what's going on here, but you do." I prayed for a few moments and then looked at her and asked, "Do you know anyone who is a person of faith, someone who believes the Bible?"

Again, she gave me a nod.

"Can you talk with him or her about what's going on?"

She agreed to do so. I prayed one more time for specific guidance and wisdom, then smiled and said good-bye.

As I left the store, I remember being surprised by how tangible the presence of the Holy Spirit had been during the whole encounter. After a few steps, this thought hit me: *What if that was the most important thing I will ever do?* I was stunned at the idea. Immediately I countered: *What about all the preaching? The writing? The counseling?*

My mind started to wander, and I began playing possible scenarios in my mind. What if that girl was going to have an abortion and our encounter had altered her decision? And what if she has the baby and he grows up to be a believer and marries a wonderful gal? Then they have a baby who grows up and goes on a short-term missions trip to Argentina and wins a young girl to Christ, who later becomes a kind of Mother Teresa to Argentina, battling sickness and poverty and influencing tens of thousands of people to have faith in Jesus Christ?

And what if I'm standing before God one day and he brings up the people who came to Christ in Argentina, and he says, "And you know who is responsible for these folks being here today?"

I see myself curiously wondering, who?

"Ed Gungor!" God exclaims.

I'm flummoxed. "How can that be? I've never even been to Argentina?"

God replies, "Do you remember that day in Successories . . . ?"

I'm not saying anything like that happened or will happen, but what if that's the way God does things? What if the way God uses us is more covert than we could ever imagine? It's not that the work we do intentionally has no relevance; it does. But what if our best is unleashed by things that are seemingly small and insignificant?

What if God often uses an everyday life well lived as a backdrop for one act of obedience that changes the course of history?

Part of a Greater Story

Is it possible that more is going on than we can possibly understand? The apostle Paul claimed that God's paths—his schemes—are "beyond tracing out."[8] That implies some mystery. Other texts claim that each of us has a destiny—that you and I are planned, on-purpose beings whom God wanted to cast in his unfolding play. If this is true, we can't think about life in terms of making our own stories. Instead, we must each find our place in the story being told by God. If that's true, this is a world where God has a purpose and a place for everything. Then success and fulfillment are not based on personal aggrandizement or actualization but on obediently finding the positions predestined for us by God.

I saw a stage play once in which one of the minor actors had a hard time with his part. He felt he should have had a larger role, so he ended up trying to expand his bit part into a bit more. He walked on and off the stage in an exaggerated way, and his lines were stretched and out of cadence with the other actors'. Instead of lending what talent he had to the overall good of the show, his performance hurt the production. Successful acting isn't about whether you are noticed or if you have the largest part but whether you play the role you are asked to play in a way that fulfills the writer's vision and the director's instructions.

If we dare to buy into the idea that we are part of God's story, this becomes a world where small and great are irrelevant. Oh, small and great still exist— some folks will always be amazingly bright and talented stars while others of us are more like bit actors—but what difference does it make as long as both are essential? We remain different, but none is insignificant.

What if each of us fits critically into God's plan, like some kind of domino scheme?

Some time ago I watched a CNN human-interest piece on a guy in Japan who had set up one million dominoes in a large field house. As thousands of spectators gathered to watch and the cameras were rolling, he knocked over the first domino, and the fun began. It took a long time for all the dominoes to tumble, one hitting the next. I remember thinking, *What if someone had snuck in and pulled a domino or two out of line? How frustrating would that have been?*

But isn't that exactly what we do to God all the time? Because we don't take ourselves seriously, because we don't think we matter, we step out of the game. We slack off and shrink back. I wonder how many times God is left grieving because we don't accurately evaluate who we are. We waste our lives, forcing him to come up with new strategies and new people to set in place for future gestures of redemption in the field house of life. Just because we appear to have a minor role doesn't mean it isn't a critical one.

An ancient story from the writings of Theodoret, bishop of Cyrrhus in Syria in the fifth century, tells about a monk named Telemachus who arrived in Rome from the East. Not much is known about him. He was not a famous theologian or church leader. He was an everyday monk.

The Roman emperor of the day was Honorius, who ruled from AD 395 to 423. Honorius was a Christian and did much to promote Christianity. But he did not take any action to eliminate the carryover from bloodthirsty pagan days, the so-called "games" of the gladiators.

The story goes that one afternoon in AD 404, Telemachus went to the Colosseum to see what the popular gladiatorial games were all about. When he witnessed two of the gladiators hacking each other to bits as the blood-drunk crowd egged them on, he was horrified. Unwilling to stand it any longer, he rushed down from the spectator seats, vaulted the arena wall, ran over to the combatants, and tried to separate them before they could further harm each other.

When the mob saw what was happening, they went wild. They did not approve of Telemachus's love for life; they were infuriated by it. Many angry spectators surged into the arena, grabbed stones, and pelted the monk until he lay dead. He was murdered as he tried to stop the senseless death of others in the name of entertainment.

A little-known monk who devoted his whole life to

the simple service of God was silenced when he dared lift his voice against the madness of institutionalized murder. But that wasn't the end of the story.

Honorius heard of the tragic event and recognized the need to stop those savage games. He hailed the monk as a Christian martyr, and in AD 404 he issued a decree forbidding all gladiatorial games thereafter. Though it would be some time before the games were stopped altogether, one act by a little-known Christ-follower changed the known world. January 1 on the Christian calendar remains a feast day that honors Saint Telemachus for his sacrifice.

The Bible is chock-full of stories that exemplify the idea that the obedience of one seemingly insignificant person can change the world. Here's one: A young woman named Ruth leaves her family and the land of her birth to care for the mother of her dead husband. Ruth is a Moabite woman; Naomi, her mother-in-law, is an Israelite. But Ruth is immovable in her selfless dedication to Naomi. She tells her, "Where you go I will go, and where you stay I will stay. Your people will be my people and your God my God."[9] When Ruth arrives in Israel with Naomi, the two women are destitute. At Naomi's urging, Ruth marries this guy who is twice her age, just to survive (the tone of the text suggests he was not an Abercrombie & Fitch model). The story ends with Ruth's giving birth to a son named Obed. Nice story, but that's about it.

Though the story of Ruth is sweet from one standpoint, it's so ordinary—so seemingly unimportant. But then we are surprised: Ruth, it turns out, is the great-grandmother of David, the greatest king in Israel's history, a man after God's own heart.[10] The dedication and selfless love David showed in his life mirror the same selfless commitments his great-grandmother Ruth had. I'll bet when Ruth met David in heaven and realized the connection to such a pivotal person in God's plan, she was shocked. I'm sure she had no idea she was such a central player in God's kingdom enterprise.

What if this is God's MO? What if God loves to weave the spectacular from ordinary thread? And what if he loves to do it in a way that most people miss—unless they're suspicious? Maybe being suspicious about God's activity is what faith really is.

Forgetting Big

Forget about big. Abandon your longing for the spectacular. Fall in love with life—the everyday, normal kind. The beauty of a small dog is that he doesn't worry about being small. He's ready to take on the world. We ordinary humans can—and should—follow suit. Remember, small is the new big. We need to challenge the notion that earthly prominence, status, beauty, power, and wealth are essential for one to matter. Those misleading notions have polluted the way we see ourselves long enough.

Those who hope for big are usually in a mad dash for significance and destiny and end up destroying much of the good in their lives. Often they finish with nothing more than an oversized ego and a world of fantasy. Most people who talk big don't end up big; many are just obnoxious big-dog wannabes. If God really has something big in store for you, you'll likely achieve it through small actions anyway.

So, how does this work? How does a small dog matter if he never makes the evening news? Being small doesn't get all that much good press. The big dogs always steal the show; they get the ribbons, the trophies, the big write-ups in the paper. The small dogs don't. But smart small dogs know how to use smallness to bring about huge changes in the world.

We need to learn how to embrace small in a culture that only celebrates big. We turn to that next.

Chapter 2

Fight the
Big-Dog Lie

M Y SMALL DOG, FRANK, BENEFITS from a huge gift he didn't have to work for—it just comes naturally. The gift is that Frank knows exactly who he is. If you knew him, you'd probably agree that Frank is not an unusually handsome dog. And, as I've already pointed out, he's not a big, strong, impressive dog. But if Frank is aware of being a little south of grand, you'd never guess it. He carries an air of self-confidence.

I want to be more like Frank. I don't want to accept the lie that I'm nothing more than what others say I am. If my place in life is that of a small dog, why should I accept that anything else could be better for me?

Frank may never come away with a trophy for Best in Show. But I haven't noticed his losing any sleep over it. It seems he knows far better than I that it isn't all about size, beauty, and power. In fact, his demeanor screams that external measures are meaningless as indicators of true value. Small dogs like Frank don't believe the big-dog lie.

The Big-Dog Lie: Bigger Is Better

The world tells us this lie all the time—and we tend to believe it. Let's face it: the world is rigged against small dogs. Everywhere you look, big is rewarded with higher status, and small is shoved aside. We buy into the lie that "big dogs" are more valuable and matter more than we do. But we shouldn't buy it. In God's scheme of things, it's just the opposite: the last are first, the bottom is top, and small dogs like us are commissioned to change the world. A little dog stands out in the world not because she pretends to be big but because she takes seriously the truth that God uses small dogs in a big way.

What if God intended for there to be those who are

more and those who are less, some who are flashy and some who aren't so arresting? Perhaps a big part of faith is resisting the judgments people make about those differences—even when we land on the losing side of their judgments. The idea that we are smaller than others elicits some pretty horrid feelings in our psyches. Maybe we're *not* good enough. We start asking ourselves, *Do I matter? Am I okay?* But the answers tend only to affirm our sense of insecurity and insignificance—and we rebel against them, because we all want to matter; we all need to matter. Nothing is more basic than that.

But what if worth isn't supposed to be determined by how we compare with others? What if we shouldn't be intimidated or feel put down because we're smaller than others and they outshine us in various ways? And who's to say that what people judge to be better than something else is even accurate?

I love the color red. But who's to say that red is better than green—or blue, or yellow, or all the shades in between? What if green felt bad about itself because it wasn't blue, or what if yellow cowered in shame because it wasn't red, or orange hid in fear because it wasn't a primary color? Don't all colors add to the whole of the experience of life?

I recently saw a huge painting of a rich chocolate

liquid with what looked like the top of a dark red cherry swimming in it. The red was the smallest color on the painting, but its contrast was stunning. The little dab of red made the whole image work for me. What if the little dab of red tried to cover itself up because it was smaller than the rich brown that dominated the painting?

Small isn't less important than big; it's just different. We wouldn't even know to apply a word like *small* if we didn't stop to compare one thing with another. Yet not only are comparisons invalid—worthless, in God's economy—they can be discouraging and detrimental. The apostle Paul wrote that those who "measure themselves by themselves and compare themselves with themselves" are "not wise."[1] And who wants to be unwise? When we start to believe the lie that bigger is better—that the more we have, the more valuable we are—we start doing all we can to be the greatest, look the best, be the best, and have the best. We strive to be the biggest dog in the realm. And without knowing it, we destine ourselves for failure.

As apprentices of Jesus Christ, we must consciously refuse to panic about being small in a big-dog world. In fact, we should celebrate both small and big. But accepting and even celebrating small in a culture like ours is a strange concept indeed.

The Lie of External Measures

I think we humans keep jumping the track because we're confused about what to use to measure personal value. We put way too much emphasis on external things like looks, wealth, power, position, connections, and influence. We fail to realize that the external things ultimately don't matter. Now, I don't expect you to accept that statement at face value. If you'd said the same thing to me a few years ago, I would have challenged your assertion.

Before you buy into the big-dog lie, give it careful thought. Big dogs put their confidence in things that impress other big dogs. Admittedly, such things are easy to notice, but they are external. They don't tell you who a big dog really is on the inside. It's what's inside that counts most. And there's another problem: when externals matter too much, it makes you weird.

Here's an example. The other night I watched a documentary on eating disorders. The program featured women of all ages who were struggling with the lie that unless they weighed less than one hundred pounds, they were fat. I watched as these girls obsessed about their weight, purged the food they were forced to eat by making themselves vomit, disclosed their rabid passion for exercise, and admitted compulsions like trying on dozens of outfits to find the perfect one for any given day. These girls and women were slaves to a meaningless (and extremely unrealistic) external measuring stick. In their world, the big-dog ideal was to be really, really thin. Their lives revolved around the idea that they must be a certain size to have any value. Believing this lie threatened not just their health but their very survival. It's a lie that could kill them. But they believed it.

That's how an external standard like "beauty" works. Someone decides what's beautiful and what's not, and that person or group's arbitrary decision determines who is beautiful and who is not. We're all expected to conform to the capricious standard. In some cultures the most beautiful women are tall; in others, short gals win the day. I grew up in the fifties, and the babes of that era were curvaceous, full-figured women. That didn't change until the supermodel Twiggy became popular in the sixties. I'll never forget the night she appeared on the popular TV show *Rowan & Martin's Laugh-In*. Her name was completely appropriate. She was a virtual twig, but the beauty police destined her to become the new 10.

During the Renaissance the hotties were large women. Robust. Rotund. Yet they were judged to be the perfect 10s. There is a country in Africa where guys refuse to marry women who are too thin. In that culture the families of potential brides have to place the bride-to-be in a "fattening hut." There they fill her with milk and other fattening foods to help her gain weight so the marriage won't be called off and the dowry lost. In that society, the fatter the girl, the more eligible she becomes. A news piece I watched about this culture ended with a new husband excitedly asserting that he was hoping his newly acquired bride (who had gained some forty pounds in preparation for the wedding) would gain another fifty or even one hundred pounds in the months to come! "One hundred pounds would make me very happy!" he exclaimed to the camera crew.

Okay.

Obviously, beauty is in the eye of the beholder. One of the ancient kings of Israel was quite fond of women. You could say he was the all-time world champion record holder when it came to enjoying women. His problem was he couldn't stop enjoying women. Solomon had a thousand women in his harem, and I'm not speaking figuratively. He said his gang of gals was filled with "the delights of the heart of man."[2] When he describes his favorite wife in the Song of Songs, he lists the physical features that made this woman the perfect 10 of his day. (Remember, she beat out 999 other gloriously beautiful women.) Her nose was like the "tower of Lebanon" (apparently small-nosed women weren't deemed gorgeous). Her neck was like an "ivory tower" (giraffe woman?).[3] Her breasts were "like two fawns"[4] (I guess that culture avoided breast augmentation). And get this: her waist was like a "mound of wheat."[5] No washboard abs on this gal. She wouldn't be allowed anywhere near a Miss Universe pageant today, but she got Solomon's motor running.

The point of comparing such contradictory definitions of beauty is that all varieties of physical appearance have been around since the dawn of time. Cultures simply assign some people the role of beautiful and others the role of ugly. The Twiggys who lived during the Renaissance went unnoticed. Many robust women of today are ignored as well (unless your address is somewhere in Africa).

It's important to recognize that beauty is subjective. On what basis can we claim one person is more beautiful than another? No standard for beauty has held true for all time in all places. Cultural valuations of beauty are arbitrary at best. Sadly, these arbitrary values can have devastating results. The culture of beauty that pervades the West causes girls, women (and now even growing numbers of men) to hate the way they look and to work hard to develop the traits that supposedly make them beautiful. This fosters everything from eating disorders to spending a fortune on radical cosmetic surgery—not to mention that the individuals who buy into these false values are often left living false, superficial lives.

The truth is, every woman is beautiful. If you study cultural anthropology, you'll find that at some time in history, somewhere in the world, every shape, size, and look has been a 10. If you don't happen to fit today's definition of beautiful, that only means the definition is faulty. It says nothing about who you are, what your value is, or for what you are destined.

Today's definition of physical beauty is just one of the many ways external standards are used to measure us, rank us, and assign us a role and identity in the world. You might be concerned about how your salary compares to the next guy's, how the car you drive measures up, or the prestige of your title at work. Even if you've overcome the beauty lie, you still might struggle with wanting your kids to achieve more, hoping the house you live in compares favorably to others', the perceived embarrassment of not being able to afford the cruises your friends seem to go on every year, or why you haven't been invited to join a certain club.

None of us has to look hard to find yet another measurement, standard, or basis for comparison that our culture uses to impress on us that we're not worth very much. And sadly, too many of us spend our lives trying to get people to see that we do measure up, that we are important and influential and better than others. If you buy into this, you are buying into a lie. And as long as you believe that lie, you will hate your life.

Real Value

So if our worth isn't determined by our size, our beauty, or any other external measurement, what does govern our value? How do we determine our significance? What am I worth? What are you worth? These are huge questions, and the answers are vital. Deep inside, we all fear that we're not worth very much (yes, even the big dogs). And if we are in fact worthless, then life has no meaning. These fears press in on us, causing us to doubt ourselves and dread life.

Why can't we instead prance around like Frank, buoyed by a sense of self-confidence that comes with simply being alive? The Bible supports the idea that if you're alive, you matter—and you matter just as much as anyone else on the planet. Externals are not factored in to the equation. In fact, the Bible says just the opposite: each person matters because God made him or her. God formed us long before we were out walking around, wearing cool clothes and doing our best to impress somebody.

You Are Needed

Leo Buscaglia wrote:

> There is a wonderful fable that tells of a young girl who is walking through a meadow when she sees a butterfly impaled upon a thorn. Very carefully she releases it and the butterfly starts to fly away. Then it comes back and changes into a beautiful good fairy. "For your kindness," she tells the little girl, "I will grant you your fondest wish." The little girl thinks for a moment and replies, "I want to be happy." The fairy leans toward her and whispers in her ear and then suddenly vanishes.
>
> As the girl grew, no one in the land was more happy than she. Whenever anyone asked her for the secret of her happiness, she would only smile and say, "I listened to the good fairy."
>
> As she grew quite old, the neighbors were afraid the fabulous secret might die with her. "Tell

us, please," they begged, "tell us what the fairy said." The now lovely old lady simply smiled and said, "She told me that everyone, no matter how secure they seemed, had need of me."[6]

You will know your real value and not fear being small if you understand that God created you in such a way that others actually need you. Mother Teresa said, "We ourselves feel that what we are doing is just a drop in the ocean. But the ocean would be less because of that missing drop."[7]

Scripture holds that each of us is born into God's world of plenitude—the world is his stage, and we are participants in his play. The psalmist said, "Know that the LORD is God. It is he who made us, and we are his."[8] The saints who have gone before us understood that success and fulfillment are not the results of personal initiative or finding your way as an individual but of finding the place predestined for you by God.

The you-need-to-be-a-big-dog-to-matter story leads one to believe that worth is determined by beauty, money, position, et cetera. If that's true, then we are compelled to do all we can to get as much of that stuff as possible. The world becomes a place for taking, a field of competition, a place for one-upping, overcoming, conquering; a place where only the fittest survive. This kind of world perpetuates the anxiety of wondering just how fit we are and if our fit is fit enough. In this kind of world, popularity polls matter, youth matters, beauty matters; the poor, the weak, the unbeautiful, the handicapped, the aged, and those less than perfect 10s are discarded and forgotten.

The questions—Who am I? What am I? Why am I here? Do I matter? Am I making a difference? Will anyone remember me when I'm gone?—have differing answers depending on which story you choose to believe about what's going on around you. If the Bible is true, it impacts everything. We become front-page material for God's news. And if this is true, it means that the story that claims you must be outstanding to matter is a myth.

Which story do you believe?

It is confidence in the God story that affords us the security of knowing that we matter. And since God created us to matter, we can deduce that this world is in need of us. And just as the good fairy understood, knowing you are needed is one of the great secrets to happiness in this life.

It's about Service,
Not Stardom

In the 1800s Antoine Frédéric Ozanam, founder of the Society of St. Vincent de Paul, whose members worldwide still care for the material and spiritual welfare of impoverished people, wrote: "Philanthropy is a vain woman for whom good actions are a piece of jewelry and who loves to look at herself in the mirror. Charity [on the other hand] is a tender mother who keeps her eyes fixed on the infant she carries at her breast, who no longer thinks of herself, and who forgets her beauty for her love."[9]

When it comes to church ministry, many in the church are philanthropists: telling others how to be forgiven or "helped" becomes a little piece of jewelry we gaze at in the mirror. There we see how wonderful we are for being willing to tell folks what's wrong with them and right with us. We don't nurse the hurting—we don't touch them at all; that's way too intimate. We separate from them and judge them. We don't brush their faces and kiss their foreheads; we don't take the risk of holding them, of caring for them.

Maybe that's why the West is now referred to as a post-Christian culture.

And in response to the rejection of Christianity by

our culture, we rush to fix our image and change our culture by creating our own sick version of the popular *American Idol* TV talent show by underwriting slick, high-impact ministers who ultimately model talent over compassion and performance over servanthood.

I think that's sad. And we shouldn't let it stay this way. But we do so because we have inflated the concept of "ministry" to the point where it's more about the minister and his or her gifts than it is about those who are in need. And we are way too tolerant of the expectations of those leaders who feed on being seen and being important. We give them the special honor they demand because we see them as more vital to the cause of Christ than we are.

That's wrong. I contend that God cares as much about stay-at-home moms as he does about missionaries on the front lines in Bangladesh. He cares as much for a young couple working through stuff during their first year of marriage as he does for a church staff working out how to implement a small-group ministry in a church setting. He cares as much about what's going on in your life on Monday morning as he does about what goes on in the pulpit on Sunday morning. Those who think differently are not thinking biblically.

In writing about the gifts and abilities of individuals in the church, Paul showed that God takes a special interest in everyday, ordinary people—those whose gifts appear weaker. He wrote: "Those parts of the body that seem to be weaker are indispensable."[10] He said later that God purposefully "has given greater honor to the parts that lacked it."[11] Think of that. God gives special honor to what others consider common. Why does he do this? Paul said it's "so that there should be no division in the body, but that its parts should have equal concern for each other."[12]

The church is to be a community of equals. Sure, some have public, standout gifts of communication or musicianship, but those gifts don't entitle them to be treated as more important than others. We can't take the credit or the honor for our gifts: we did not create them in ourselves. Paul wrote, "Who makes you different from anyone else? What do you have that you did not receive? And if you did receive it, why do you boast as though you did not?"[13]

Maybe we should stop making Christians celebrities and start looking for the unique value and plan God has for each person within the community of faith. Maybe God wants to express himself through the common in ways we have ignored.

Sacred Spaces

When I first began pastoring twenty-five years ago, I spent the bulk of my time studying, praying, and counseling people. I lived and breathed ministry and longed for the spectacular. Whatever was going to happen, I knew it was going to be large. My ego, my expectations, and my plans grew exponentially by the minute. (I could almost hear the roar of the private jet God was sending my way.)

Though I loved my family with all my heart, I had a difficult time justifying casual time with them. My greatest dread was my day off. That was a day I was to stay home and do the regular stuff—nonbig stuff. Although my wife, Gail, looked forward to these days, they were like a scourge to me. I would rather be praying, preparing, and setting strategies to affect the world at large than taking out the trash, tumbling on the floor with our toddler, or going shopping at the mall with Gail. On those days I often exasperated her because, though I was with her physically, she sensed that I was somewhere else mentally and emotionally. I was tons of fun.

I knew God expected me to "service" my relationship with my family, and I really loved them. But it seemed to me that God valued ministry over garbage removal, playtime, and casual chatter—and he certainly didn't care about shopping. There was never any question that if someone needed me to pray, counsel, or preach at him, I must lay my day off "on the altar" to follow God's call.

Then came the day in the spring of 1982 that would forever change the way I saw things.

I woke up late that morning and didn't get my regular prayer and study time in before the family was up and about. I knew that if I ran off to study and pray then, it would look to Gail like another workday. So I stayed home and started participating in what was happening around the house (though I was disappointed and a little short on patience for not getting my devotional time).

I kept mentally beating myself, thinking, *I should have gotten up earlier! How can I expect to win the world for Christ if I'm not consistent in my devotional time?*

Then I would catch myself: *Forget it for now, Edwin. You're supposed to focus on family stuff now—you can pray later.*

By noon I had helped clean the house; had coffee and conversation with Gail; and fed, changed, and started rocking Michael, our firstborn, to sleep for his midday nap. Gail also decided to take a nap. As the nap window opened, I smelled opportunity. I thought to myself, *All right! I can run and spend some time with the Lord.*

Actually, by this point I was somewhat proud of myself. I had been a pretty good husband and father all morning, and now I was ready to press in and be a good Christian too.

After Michael fell asleep, I laid him down and hastened toward the stairs, excited that I could finally work in my God time. As I passed our bedroom, I heard Gail call to me, "Honey, would you please rub the back of my neck?" She had a headache.

My reaction wasn't good. I bristled inside. *Doesn't she appreciate all I've done today?* I thought. *I'm a pastor . . . a spiritual leader . . . God's man. I need time with God!*

I knew she had the right to ask for attention, but this wasn't the right time. I had fulfilled my natural duties all day long. It was time to me to be about my Father's business.

Just as I was about to protest, I heard a kind of gentle knocking going on deep within my heart. And I sensed these words: *If you'll do this, I will show you something.* I understood it to be the voice of God.

I was puzzled: here I was in the midst of frustration and feeling selfish about my life, and I was hearing God's voice. *Okay,* I said in my thoughts to him. As I began to massage Gail's neck, the unexpected happened—the very presence of God filled our room. Thoughts raced in different directions through my mind: *What's happening? Does she sense this? Why are you present like this, Lord?*

As I looked at Gail, she seemed more beautiful than ever. This presence seemed to make me appreciate her more. I loved massaging her neck and just being with her. It seemed important and valuable. I had been heading for study and prayer—surely that was more important in God's eyes than spending more time with the girl I had married . . . or was it? What was going on?

The Bible talks about something called the anointing. The term implies an "upon" presence of the Holy Spirit. *Upon* suggests the idea of pressure from above. The anointing is an action of God in which he comes upon individuals and they are enabled or empowered to do things they could not have done without him.

I was familiar with God's presence (or anointing) in various areas of my life. As a preacher, I often sensed his presence as I spoke. In counseling sessions, a wave of insight would come, and I knew it was God equipping me to give wise counsel. Many times, when praying for sick or troubled people, I have sensed a strong anointing of God that emboldened my faith for more effective prayer. In sharing my faith with others, I have experienced God's palpable presence helping me say things I didn't plan to say or even realize I knew. But I had never experienced God's presence or anointing to be a husband. I thought I was to do that alone. I never imagined that God cared about something so domestic.

On that day with Gail, the Holy Spirit was anointing me, enabling me to be sensitive to my wife's needs. But it was more than that.

The unusual thing here was that God was helping me to do something everyday—something totally common. He was helping me meet my wife's needs just as he had always anointed me to preach the gospel or communicate life to hurting people. This screamed to me that God actually cares about my life—my boring, mundane, everyday, nonbig life. And it changed everything for me. I began to see that my everyday life was not just the stuff of duty: it qualified to be a place for infatuation with the holy—sacred space where God's life could be expressed as much as through any other "spiritual" place (or maybe that every place qualifies as spiritual).

I can't help but wonder what would happen if the whole body of Christ began to think this way. If this idea is true, the church really is a sleeping giant. One could readily understand why Satan would never want us to discover this. He would want us to think we need to have "all the kingdoms of the world and their splendor"[14] if we want to change the world (as he tried to convince Jesus). But we don't have to be big dogs jacked up with all kinds of power and authority in order to change the world. Somehow Jesus enters the unpowerful, authority-challenged "ordinary" and releases the kingdom of God through it.

Could it be that God has secretly positioned his church in ordinary places all over the world in the hope that we will seize those places as beachheads for his kingdom? Some of the most significant things done by organizations and governments are accomplished covertly. Many of our most powerful government agencies, like the CIA, FBI, and NSA, are covert. And those who work undercover have power precisely because no one knows who they are. The agencies that break up crime find power in secrecy. Their agents don't have a public face. Their identities are hidden. It is to their advantage to come across as normal and unremarkable as they can. That's when they can best fit in and do their undercover work.

What if God has strategically placed believers all over the world without much "public face"? The Bible says, "The secret things belong to the Lord."[15] Maybe we are naive to think we are only moms or dads, only maids or taxi drivers, only waiters or mechanics. What if there are no "onlys" with God? What if we are all undercover for him as we take on the kingdom of darkness and call people "to open their eyes and turn them from darkness to light, and from the power of Satan to God"[16]? As his undercover agents, we can sneak under the radar into friendships and relationships with people from every segment of society—both high and low. Our goal? To communicate love, encourage true beauty, and fight for justice until the whole earth is "filled with the knowledge of the glory of the LORD, as the waters cover the sea."[17] Nice.

Maybe becoming content with being small, and wise about exploiting the space small affords, is more critical in God's economy of thought than our trying to elect a "Christian" president or finding the next Billy Graham we can shove onto television or building the biggest church campus in town.

Scripture supports the idea that God, since the beginning of time, has tried to break into the world through the ordinary lives of the devoted. Sadly, few of us have taken him seriously. Most can't grasp, *God wants to use me*. We think, *Not me*. We feel too insignificant, too small. We are scandalized by our own ordinariness. But God loves to flash the eternal into ordinary life and release his kingdom through people and circumstances that appear small. God seems to do his best work in hidden, secret, small places—in the home, in the womb, in the heart.

Fall in love with the ordinary. Dare to believe that the minor details of your life matter to God. Dare to believe that you're not a mistake. Besides, being ordinary and small may actually be evidence that God took extra time to make you that way. Why? Because being small sets you up to fit in places that big cannot.

Let's take a look at that next.

Chapter 3

Dare to Be Small

OUR DOG, FRANK, IS A Westie. Cute dog. You'd recognize his breed from the packaging of Cesar brand dog food or as one of the mascots for Black & White (a brand of Scotch whiskey). Westies grow to be only ten to eleven inches high at the shoulder and weigh less than twenty pounds. We love that Frank is small. He can zoom around and play fetch in the house, jump up on our laps, ride in the car, lie on the ottoman right next to our feet—all with ease. Great Danes, German shepherds, mastiffs, and the like can't do all that—they're the big dogs. I'm sure there are some advantages that come with big dogs, but for the Gungor family, small dogs are best.

Often, small is a better fit than big.

Years ago, when my daughter, Elisabeth, was little, I was cleaning out a car I was trading in. As I checked under the driver's seat for any leftover treasure, I saw a music cassette tape nestled in a place I had never noticed (those bucket seats were close to the floor). I got on my knees and started reaching for the tape. To my chagrin, the bottom of the seat was hungry for flesh and started digging into my forearm as I reached for the prize. I could just barely touch the tape and succeeded only in pushing it deeper underneath the seat. Undaunted, I tried to force my arm in farther. But that only made matters worse as the fatter part of my forearm met with the same tiny space.

My daughter watched me struggle for a few moments before she started pulling on my shirt to get my attention.

"Daddy," she said, peeking over my shoulder into the car.

"Just a minute, honey," I responded, intent on bagging my prey.

"Daddy," she said a little more urgently.

"Hold on," I said insistently. "I'm trying to get this tape."

"Daddy!" she said, nearly hollering.

I sat upright and snapped, "What do you want?"

She leaned past me, slid her little arm under the seat, and easily snagged what I was nearly committing suicide to get. After she handed me the tape and skipped off, I remember thinking, *Little fits where big doesn't.*

There really are places where big isn't best and where little wins the day.

Loving Small

So how does one embrace small in a culture so enamored with and controlled by big? Well, it's not easy. But it helps if we remember a few things about what God was doing when he created us small.

Small by Design

Christian theism holds that if one is less than someone else in terms of talent or intelligence or beauty, etc., then God created the person that way with purpose. The psalmist saw it: "I am fearfully and wonderfully made,"[1] he exclaimed. Being okay with being less is no small matter; it takes lots of courage. But that courage finds its root in the idea that God made each of us a certain way in order to fulfill a role he has for each of us in his story.

The Bible helps us understand that each person was calibrated by God to fit in this world where he wanted each one of us to fit. Your personality—what makes you laugh, what makes you feel loved, how you make decisions, etc.—was purposefully designed. Your talents and abilities (or lack of them) all play into God's fitting you into specific places on earth for specific times to reach specific people (see Acts 17:26).

This is a cool idea if you happen to be as good-looking as Ben Affleck or Julia Roberts; or if you're as talented as Sting or Bono. But what if you aren't? What if you're kind of ugly, by media standards? What if you can't sing? What if you can't speak well in front of people or you aren't very smart? What if you have what some would call a birth defect? What if your uniqueness is a small uniqueness—it only stands out after people get to know you? Is that evidence that you're some kind of mistake, or is it possible that God made you that way on purpose?

The psalmist speaks of the "small and great alike."[2] What if God made some of us small intentionally? We fear the idea of being small in our culture, but what if God doesn't agree? What if, in God's economy of thought, big isn't always best? What if small is often the best alternative through which to influence the world? That would sure explain some things.

Small but Complex

How do you feel when you encounter someone who is bigger than life or stunningly talented? When I meet great people, most often I feel like less. It's a bit like visiting the Grand Canyon—big things have a way of making you feel a tad insignificant. When you witness amazing people, you tend to feel unamazing by comparison. These big dogs don't inspire you to be what you can be; they proudly show you all *they* can be—leaving you paralyzed in the certainty that you will never be as good as they are, so why try?

True, God has chosen to create such amazing people. And instead of falling prey to envy, we should celebrate those folks. But we should never believe that amazing people somehow diminish those of us who don't seem to be. The truth is, amazing doesn't fit everywhere. Amazing, standout people are too big—too overpowering—to network with others who shine best when they're part of a team. God has prepared a significant role for everyday, ordinary people. And if you really stop to think about it, an argument can be made that making people ordinary and less talented or less gifted or less brilliant might actually take more creative effort on God's part. Let me explain.

Small is often amazing. If you've been around for the past thirty years, you've likely been stupefied at the progress made in the personal computing world. Engineers have tackled the seemingly impossible task of jamming more and more data and processing speed into tiny microchips. They have found a way to get the power of computers that used to fill whole rooms into chips that fit in your hand. And guess what? Those same engineers claim that the big stuff was much easier to create than the small stuff.

My boys were young when the toy company Galoob first came out with their Micro Machines. Those things were so cool. I couldn't get over the striking detail of the tiny cars and trucks. It's difficult to create small things with moving, functioning parts.

So, here's a thought: what if creating people with small talent and small ability requires a greater miracle than making the big, talented, brainy people? Is it possible that it takes God more power to create something that is less?

Just ask a professional singer to sing out of tune; it's tough to do. She'll probably say that it's harder for her to sing poorly than to sing well. Could a similar thing be true for God? What if it's harder to make things less great when all you are is great?

Imagine standing on a beach and being hit by a seventy-foot tidal wave. The instant before the wave hits, you close your eyes, expecting to be swept away. Instead, as the monstrous wave passes, you are left standing on the shore with only one drop of moisture on your forehead. How could so much water leave so little of itself? What would you say? You would exclaim, "It's a miracle!"

Okay. So how does the only omnipotent Being in the universe, who is perfect and powerful and brilliant, creatively splash a person into existence who can't sing or dance or tackle math with ease? That had to be tough. Maybe small is the greatest miracle of all.

Small but Mighty

We've seen that small serves a purpose in God's plan, and that small can be amazingly complex, but did you know small can be incredibly powerful too? As modern warfare developed, scientists tried to build bigger and bigger bombs. But some of them began to suspect that the greatest power would be found in the smallest place—the atom. And sure enough, when they figured out how to release the potential inherent in that particular bit of small, it unleashed a staggering, never-before-seen power. It turned out that an incredible amount of power really did reside in the smallest place.

If only the church of Jesus Christ would learn that lesson. I wonder if the church is continuing to lose ground in our culture because we keep looking for the next Billy Graham or Mother Teresa—for the "big bombs." Is it possible that the greatest power for God's kingdom is found in the small, in the lives of everyday, common people—the laity?

Author Dallas Willard writes:

> If [Jesus] were to come today as he did then, he could carry out his mission through most any decent and useful occupation. He could be a clerk or accountant in a hardware store, a computer repairman, a banker, an editor, doctor, waiter, teacher, farmhand, lab technician, or construction worker. He could run a house-cleaning service or repair automobiles. In other words, if he were to come today he could very well do what you do. He could very well live in your apartment or house, hold down your job, have your education and life prospects, and live within your family, surroundings, and time. None

of this would be the least hindrance to the eternal kind of life that was his by nature and becomes available to us through him.[3]

Don't you find it curious that Jesus didn't enter into the world as royalty or as a famous scholar or wealthy merchant? He could have chosen to occupy a station in life that afforded some glitz, glamour, status, and authority. Why pick tiny Nazareth and a splinter-filled carpentry career for the backdrop of his life? Doesn't a life destined to change the whole world demand something less common? Yet commonplace is precisely the stage upon which God chooses to reveal and express his life. In the final analysis, it seems God loves to use what we call ordinary in some special, mysterious way.

The Chosen

If you want to embrace small, recognize that you are chosen. The Bible tells us that before time—in eternity—God imagined you. This means he manipulated the odds through history to make sure you got here.

Do you have any idea what the odds were against your showing up? Human males produce around 700 million sperm a day. Human females only produce about four hundred mature eggs in an entire lifetime. So, think about it: one particular day, the sperm that ended up being half of you had to beat the other 700 million to that rare mature female egg so you could have a shot at life. If you calculate the odds of your parents' picking the day you were formed to get romantic, which also happened to be the day your mom had a mature egg in place—the odds against your being the one to make it to be conceived and born shoots to something like 255,500,000,000 billion to one (any lottery gives you much better odds).

To make matters even more improbable, consider the odds stacking higher and higher against your being born the further you go into your history—or all the odds your ancestors faced (your parents, their parents, their parents, and so on, right back to the first humans) that had to turn out just so in order for you to exist. In each generation every parent, grandparent, great-grandparent, and so on—in increasing numbers—had to meet the right partner to produce the right offspring that would eventually lead to you. The fact that you are even alive is an unimaginable chance of trillions-upon-trillions to one.

To God, this isn't a land for the survival of the fittest—it's a world for the predestined. He picked us. And he has a plan for us. This means you were a forethought in God's mind; that you are not here by chance and that, in a very real way, you are a dream come true for God.

Scripture goes so far as to say that God managed your growth while you were in your mother's womb[6]— that your physicality and unique blend of personality were on purpose. You were chosen specifically to inhabit this planet. The biblical story affirms that you and I are not accidents—we are on-purpose beings God placed in the world as unique characters in his unfolding story. Understanding that you're here because you were handpicked by God will change the tone of your life and affect how you live and how you feel about yourself.

When I was a kid, I had a pretty severe case of childhood asthma. I couldn't run much, and because my dad was a Turkish immigrant who didn't play baseball or football, he never coached me to hone my skills in those regards (they remain latent to this day). So the scene usually played out like this: The gym teacher would line us all up against the wall. He'd assign two captains, and the selection would begin. All the popular kids got picked first, then the average ones. Eventually everyone had been chosen except for me and one of the girls. By this time I'd be nervously shuffling my feet, wringing my hands, and dying inside.

Then one team captain would say to the other, "You take Gungor."

"No way. I had him last time," would come the retort. "I'll take the fat girl."

Such was my life. (I think most of us have experienced the sickening feeling of not being chosen, not being wanted, not being asked to the dance.)

As I entered high school, I wasn't very popular. In fact, one upper classman hated me. I'd be walking down the hall, and he would knock my books out of my hand and onto the floor and then punch me in the stomach. I was a ninth grader, and he was a star wrestler in his junior year—way intimidating. I dreaded seeing Billy and would do whatever I could to avoid him.

One afternoon as I was walking home from school, I noticed two cars pulling up about a block away from me. I watched as a gaggle of boys jumped out of the cars, got into bowling-pin formation, and headed directly toward me. Billy was in the front-pin position. I panicked inside. But before I could come up with an escape plan, Billy was in my face. He knocked my books to the ground and started shoving me in the chest (here we go again).

"Wanna fight, Gungor?" he jeered.

"No," I answered sheepishly.

"C'mon Gungor. You a chicken?" he snapped.

I felt helpless.

But then something happened that changed my whole high-school career. Bit came to the rescue. Let me explain.

Bit was the biggest, coolest kid at Neillsville High School. He was huge and built like a rock. We all knew he had started shaving in seventh grade, which gave him legendary status. The reason we called him Bit was because he had a huge acne problem and, because of our respect, we didn't want to call him Zit.

"Billy!" Bit bellowed. "If you're going to mess with Gungor, you're going to have to go through me first!"

I can't really describe for you all that happened in my soul at that moment. The coolest kid in the school had just sided with me! My fear, my anxiety, my dread about Billy all gave way to the joy of being chosen, being valued by another. My stock value shot up instantly in my own mind (and with the crowd that had gathered around to see the fight). I had done nothing to earn this; it was Bit's kindness, and it changed my life.

That's a microsnapshot of what the biblical story is all about. It's about God's choosing to side with those much less than himself—you and me. He did so not because we did something to earn it but because of his kindness. When someone significant chooses you, it causes his or her significance to extend to you. This is

God walking across the room in front of everyone and asking you to dance. He chose you. He wants to be with you. Getting to know him, that's what gives us the confidence that we can matter in this world. The apostle Paul said that because of his encounter with Christ—because of his introduction into the Christ-story—he walked through life with confidence. "I have strength for all things in Christ Who empowers me," he wrote. "I am ready for anything and equal to anything through Him Who infuses inner strength into me; I am self-sufficient in Christ's sufficiency."[7]

It turns out we can make our mark in this world because of our relationship to God as Father, not just because of how well we perform for or compare with those around us. Being small is not threatening when we know we are chosen.

Being or Doing

It's hard for us to grasp the idea that we matter just because we are, not because we stand out in some unique, masterful way. Even Frank isn't loved in our family because he's the most amazing dog on the planet. Sure, he knows some cool tricks, and he does sing along when we sing (which makes us laugh), but that's not why we love him. We love him because he's Frank. He's *our* puppy—an old one, but still our puppy. And we love our puppy.

When I was about eight years old, I was playing in a Little League softball game. I was terrible. I was up to bat and swung just in time for my fingers to get slammed by the ball. I choked back my tears and set up for the next pitch. I swung again and got hit in the exact same place on my hand. I started to cry openly, which was extremely embarrassing in front of my friends. I remember running off the field in utter humiliation. My mom met me in the parking lot, grabbed my face, looked directly into my eyes, and said, "Don't you worry one bit about not doing well at baseball. You're a Gungor."

At the moment, I didn't know what she meant by that, but there was something in her voice that communicated to me that I was bigger than my performance. Her confidence in me despite my open failure felt like a healing balm flowing into me to let me know I was okay, no matter what. She made me believe that I mattered, not because of what I had done, but because of who I was. By the time I grew up enough to know that being a Gungor meant absolutely nothing at all, the healing salve had already permeated my soul—I had a healthy self-image and a strong sense of destiny that made me smile at the future. What a gift! (Thanks, Mom.)

Gail and I have always tried to communicate such unconditional love to our kids. We are wild about Michael and his wife, Lisa; Robert and his wife, Erin; David and his wife, Kate; and Elisabeth, our baby still in college. Six of them are musicians (one a concert violinist), four are songwriters, one is a dancer, one a brilliant Web designer; a couple are amazing communicators; and all of them are caring contributors to the world. They make Gail and me look like better parents than we actually are. But what they do is a small matter compared to who they are. We don't really care what they do (other than wanting them to be the best they can be). They are our kids, and that is basis enough for our love.

Back when *Life* magazine was still in circulation, I saw an article on what the grown-up children of the Kennedys and Rockefellers were doing with their lives. As I read that article, I noticed that my interest in their personal accomplishments stemmed from my interest in their pedigrees—their families of origin. What they *did* was important to me only because of *who they were*.

When President Clinton took office in 1993, an article about Chelsea Clinton appeared that fall in the sports section of *USA Today*. It featured a huge picture of her playing goalie on her private school's soccer team. I remember thinking in mocking tone, *Wow, I didn't know Chelsea Clinton was such an amazing soccer player that she would end up on the front page of the* USA Today *sports section! What a coincidence that this girl's dad is the president of the United States.* I knew she was probably not an extraordinary soccer player; she was newsworthy because of who she was. *Who* she was made *what* she did important.

What makes the God-story from Scripture so provocative is that it establishes that our meaning, our worth, our importance, comes from a much deeper place than our own capacities or efforts. It means that the richness of our lives is not found in what we see in the mirror or produce through our gifts or efforts; rather, it comes from our spiritual ancestry, our pedigree. For believers in Jesus, our pedigree is rooted in God. That's what makes our voices count. We matter because we are defined from an eternal place; we are part of something bigger than ourselves, part of a story God is telling. And in this story, our primary job is to make space for God to inhabit the world.

Buying into the idea that small matters turns out to be no small matter. Not to do so either causes you to resign yourself to the notion that you're no one in particular or forces you to enter a race to become someone or something you're not. To embrace small, on the other hand, is to enter the arena of faith—you come to believe that no matter what things look like, God has made you on purpose, and you are in some way critically connected to something greater than yourself. Thinking like this fills you with hope and expectation. It's a great way to live.

PART TWO

Shaking Things Up

> I want it said of me by those who knew me best,
> that I always plucked a thistle
> and planted a flower where I thought
> a flower would grow.
> Abraham Lincoln

I F YOU'RE HUMAN AND YOU have a measurable pulse, something in you probably wants to shake things up. You want to change things, to make a difference, to leave your mark on the world. You also want to be heard, to be noticed, to create a legacy. And you want to accomplish all this without having to become something you're not. But there's a problem. Though most of us have a core longing to better the world, we question whether we have what it takes to do so. Most of those known to us as movers and shakers are elevated because they have obvious marks of greatness—they are charismatic, gifted, confident, good looking, strong, well connected, and larger than life.

The good news is that in his teaching, Jesus often called attention to things small, even trivial—like the number of hairs on our heads, little children, lost coins, lost sheep, a mustard seed, or a poor old widow. It seems that when the kingdom of God influences us, it gives us the ability to see God in people and in experiences that the world holds in small regard or of little account—small players deemed far too ordinary to be marked by the kiss of the divine. But biblically speaking, our greatest opportunity to influence others is by participating in everyday life with the eyes of faith.

This is how we participate in God's plan—his story. We are a people with a cause. Because of this, we need not dread life. Our lives are not grim, joyless exercises in futility. Because our everyday actions are linked to the Christ story, our lives matter. For us, the little things of life—working out bumps in our marriages, raising children, spending time with an elderly parent, helping the underprivileged in developing countries, doing what we say, caring for one another—all such things become redeemed actions. They are part of something bigger than ourselves. As such, they have eschatological significance—they are part of an end God has in mind.

This is why we can be free from being defined by social forces, by the past, by our financial portfolios, by our ages, or by our beauty or success. We're part of something much grander. Our lives matter because our actions are redeemed and thus become part of a larger picture. We don't expect freedom to come to us by our loud assertions of individual independence, where we have to scratch out significance in what we do as compared to what others do.

We don't have to be afraid of being nobodies; we are linked to a true story—a God story—which means our ordinary lives are part of an extraordinary plan.

We all want to use our lives to make things better for others. We want to stir things up, to improve things. But is there a way to do so in a world crowded with big dogs and big-dog wannabes? I'm convinced there is. In spite of the fact that we live in a world with folks who are smarter, prettier, richer, and more talented than we are, there is a way for us to matter.

Anyone can change the world, and one doesn't

need to waste time beforehand trying to ratchet up his or her own personal greatness. When you examine history, it's been the everyday people who changed the world most.

People often say, "Don't sweat the small stuff." But I think God really does sweat the small stuff. I think he leads us and calls us to value and celebrate everyday little things because the little things matter; because the details are everything. Without the details, the big picture (God's ultimate will) never takes shape.

A perfect illustration of this is the work of nineteenth-century painter Georges Seurat, who is probably best known for his painting *A Sunday Afternoon on the Island of La Grande Jatte* (which actually inspired a Broadway musical called *Sunday in the Park with George*). Seurat is considered the father of pointillism, a form of art in which images are painted using tiny dots of color. Seurat's paintings are amazing to behold because, from a distance, they appear as slices of life at the park, the harbor, the opera, the circus, the beach, or in a field. But up close they're really just a collection of thousands of teeny, tiny dots—literally infinitesimal specks of color. It's only when one steps back for a more objective view that the "big picture" is revealed.

I believe this is how God works his will in our world. He uses millions of teeny, tiny dabs of obedience from the ordinary lives of believers to bring about the big picture—his dream for the world.

It's *how* we change the world that's so different from the way the big dogs do it. Big dogs have external power, authority, and public attention. Small dogs have none of these. So how do we accomplish change? We dig into that next.

Chapter 4

Holding On

OUR FAMILY'S FIRST DOG WAS a small terrier, like Frank, but he was a Border terrier with a grizzle-and-tan coat and fiercely intelligent eyes. We named him Max. And just dare to play tug-of-war with him. Max loved tug-of-war. With resolute determination he'd lock down on one end of the rope, shaking and jerking it back and forth and emitting a continuous, deep, bring-it-on growl.

Max (like most small dogs) had no concept of quit. He wanted to keep playing long after your arms tired. Often our whole family would take turns trying to wear him down, but without fail Max would outlast us all. Sometimes, in the battle, we would lift the rope till his back paws left the ground—the weight of his whole body would hang freely in midair! Yet Max still showed no sign of quitting. He just kept up that consistent, teasing growl while shaking his tail in pure pleasure. He was a persistent little guy.

Refusing to quit makes even the small dogs—or humans—win in life. It's kind of a bark of endurance, and it makes small dogs cast a large shadow.

Crashing through Quitting Points

Have you ever noticed that some people seem to succeed at everything they try? They have successful careers; they have great friendships and strong families; they're involved meaningfully in church or community activities; and they can stay in great shape physically. Then there are others who seem to falter at almost everything they do. Why is that?

When you get close to successful people in order to discover how they manage to fulfill so much of their potential, you find that they understand commitment, persistence, tenacity, and courage—they are people who hold on tight and refuse to quit. Contrariwise, when you examine those who have an embarrassing string of setbacks and personal failures, you often discover that although they often started out strong on some path or endeavor, somewhere along the way they let things slide. They're quitters.

They'll say things like, "I intended to do well in that class, but I put off doing my homework." "I just couldn't follow through with my leads." "I got disconnected and didn't spend time with my family." "I wanted to work out, but so many things popped up on the days I planned to go to the gym." And somewhere in the backs of their minds, they believe that intending to do things is sort of like doing them. But it isn't. Intention alone never wins the day. Bottom line: they let go of the rope.

The good news is, you can always pick it up again and get back in the game. But to win, you must learn to last. You need to learn how to endure.

The problem is, we live in a culture that has come to expect things instantly. We like fast diets, overnight fame, love at first sight, rapid fitness, and a dash to success that's only about a hundred yards. If we don't experience what we want in a reasonable amount of time—say a week or two—we think something is wrong. Those of us over fifty were once called the "now generation." We were known for quitting before we could reap the rewards of our endeavors—jobs, educational paths, relationships, pretty much anything complex. Why? We couldn't enjoy the rewards instantly, so we lost interest. Sadly, the generations that follow us exhibit the same impatience.

The small dog exhibits the kind of endurance that will make a difference in the world; it refuses to cash in—it pushes past quitting points. What are some of those quitting points? And how do we learn to keep going—or just hang on—when everything in us wants to give up?

Bad Starts

Everyone has a bad start now and then. But that doesn't mean the race is lost. Get back up. Keep going. You can make up lost ground over time. Always remember, life is not a sprint but a marathon.

Sprints and marathons are two distinctly different races. In a sprint, one of the most critical elements is the start. Runners practice for hours on end getting into those little blocks and busting out the very nanosecond the gun goes off. Why? Because those who falter at the start don't stand a chance of winning the race.

On the other hand, the starts of marathons are not

all that important. Most runners just stand around waiting for the gun to go off. You could fall down, have three guys run over you, then get up and still win the race. The start isn't so important; it's how you endure.

Today many people believe success in life is the result of a sprint, that the start is what's critical. In a recent season of the wildly popular TV show *American Idol*, a contestant from Minneapolis had his eye on the prize of becoming the next "Idol" with all its glitz, glamour, and idol worship. After being rejected by the judges and thus unable to advance in the competition, he stormed out of the room. With angry tears streaming down his cheeks, he blurted one or two expletives at Simon Cowell and the other judges and exclaimed to the camera, "I'm already sixteen, and I wanted to start out successful." He wanted to start out successful—not work toward it. He just couldn't comprehend how the judges dared end what he had dreamed of doing. How could those #@!$@!% judges throw a roadblock in front of his right to idol status?

There are a lot of you-owe-me-what-I-want-because-I'm-so-awesome-and-I-want-it people out there. The number of folks in our culture who feel they have the right to whatever they desire is steadily increasing. They aren't satisfied with the Declaration of Independence's affirmation of our right to the pursuit of happiness; they think happiness is their right straight off—no pursuit necessary. Surely happiness has no connection with anything as boring and marathonish as patience, determination, persistence, courage, fearlessness, steadfastness, and loyalty.

You don't do marathons quickly. You have to spread your energy output over time. Endurance is what empowers a person over the long haul. It makes you press on through what would otherwise be your quitting points. It reinterprets brick walls in your path as papier-mâché props with brick patterns. With endurance you can push through old, familiar conflict zones for the ten-thousandth time without giving up—in Energizer Bunny fashion, you just keep going and going and going . . .

Barriers

What barriers to success are blocking your way? How you respond to those barriers will determine your ability to shake things up and make a difference as a small dog. Will you let those barriers keep you from going on, or will you break through them and persevere? The difference is Grand Canyon–wide between thinking success is the result of hard work and possible for everyone and believing that success is the result of external factors available to big dogs only (like lack of social/cultural barriers, age barriers, economic barriers, educational barriers, etc.). True, favorable conditions and fewer barriers may create more opportunity and ease for some persons pursuing success than for others who do not have those factors in their favor. (An obese man or a woman with diabetes will face bigger challenges to getting in shape physically than might a person born into a family of athletes. But that doesn't mean getting in shape is impossible—it just means it will be harder.) The dangerous habit of many people is to interpret barriers as legitimate excuses to quit early—or not to try at all.

Don't misunderstand me—there are some formidable barriers in our world that are tough to overcome. Take failure. You tried and it just didn't work. Then you tried harder, and it still didn't work. Maybe you even tried your hardest, and it still didn't work. Who could blame you for quitting after all that? But if you peer into the histories of those who dared to shake up our world, you'll discover that they believed opposition ultimately worked to their benefit. Opposition challenged and taught them. It made them dig deeper and reach higher. Helen Keller said it well: "Although the world is full of suffering, it is also full of the overcoming of it."[1]

Years ago I read the story of Harold Russell, a young man who awakened in a hospital bed to discover that he had no hands. He was a sergeant paratrooper in World War II and had lost his hands during a training accident. His repeated thoughts were, *What good am I now? What can a man do without hands? My life is over.*

For weeks he lay overwhelmed with a sense of defeat. He couldn't begin to imagine going through life with steel hooks instead of hands and going out in public that way. He got to the point where he didn't care whether he lived or died.

A man by the name of Charley McGonegal visited Harold in the hospital. Charley was a veteran as well and, like Harold, had lost his hands while serving his country. He told Harold that the greatest battle he would now have to face was himself. He would have to quit feeling sorry for himself, face his loss, and adjust to it. Charley recited a quote from Ralph Waldo Emerson that he said had always helped him: "For everything you have missed, you have gained something else."

Charley told him to keep in mind that he was not crippled but merely handicapped. *Crippled* meant a person was incapable of performing proper or effective action. *Handicapped* meant he was disadvantaged or hindered but could still succeed if he worked hard enough.

A light went on for Harold. Being handicapped meant he had a chance. He kept those thoughts rolling through his mind: He was not crippled, he was handicapped—it would be difficult, but he could make it. And for everything he missed, he gained something else. These thoughts helped him move past the barrier of self-pity and gave him the courage to focus on life's possibilities. Harold went on to become a Hollywood movie star (winning two Academy Awards), a best-selling author, a motivational speaker, and a radio celebrity. He married his childhood sweetheart and achieved success beyond many of his contemporaries.

He wrote of those early years:

I think it was Emerson who said that a man's weakness is often his greatest strength. Waking up in a hospital bed at Camp Mackall to find that I had no hands, I wasn't quite ready to believe that. But in the years since then I have discovered and rediscovered that truth over and over again.

There is nothing startlingly new in that, I know. It is a truism as old as man, nor was Emerson the first to state it, I'm sure. Yet it is a stark fact that can be, that must be, repeated constantly so long as there are human beings on this earth. In one way or another, each of us must pass through the fires at least once in his lifetime. Each of us must find out for himself that his handicaps, his failures and shortcomings must be conquered or else he must perish.

My weakness—my handlessness—my sense of inferiority—has turned out to be my greatest strength. I didn't think so at the time it happened and I don't think I'd ever willingly lose my hands, if I had to do it all over again. But having lost them, I feel perhaps I have gained many fine things I might never have had with them. But that is not the important thing. The important thing is that this seeming disaster has brought me a priceless wealth of spirit that I am sure I could never have possessed otherwise. It is not what you have lost, but what you have left that counts.[2]

We can't control what happens to us. We can either stay down for the count after we've been pummeled and be carried out of the ring, or we can (by God's grace) pull ourselves back up to our feet and keep going.

Fatalism

An old story tells of two brothers, Bill and Tom, who grew up together on the family farm. Both boys decided to stay on and work the farm as a career. Though Tom was younger, it seemed everything he did ended in success. He was well liked, received honors in high school, got a full scholarship to a university, got his degree in agriculture, married his childhood sweetheart, and had a wonderful marriage and a couple of beautiful kids. It seemed Tom could do no wrong.

Bill, on the other hand, didn't fair nearly as well. In fact, he struggled in everything. He did poorly in school and never went to college. Bill's personal and social skills were underdeveloped. He did marry, but the marriage ended in a nasty and painful divorce. Everything he touched seemed to fall apart.

By the time Bill and Tom were both in their fifties, Tom had quite naturally taken over the management of the farm, while Bill was little more than a hired hand.

One fateful day, while Bill was plowing the fields for spring planting, a tire fell off the tractor, and the tractor tipped over and crushed him. As Bill was close to breathing his last breath, he cried out to God. "God," he begged, "why? Why have you made life so easy for Tom and so difficult for me?"

Suddenly a voice thundered from heaven: "I don't know, Bill, there's just something about you that ticks me off."

As silly as that story sounds, it isn't far from how people view why what happens to them happens. Many think God (or some kind of natural law) is responsible for our success or failure—that human effort is, for the most part, inconsequential. People of faith can be the worst about believing that whatever is destined to be will just be—no personal effort needed. They think humans have little to do with the future, that it's primarily God's domain.

Things only happen, these folks contend, because of God's sovereignty; human beings don't really cause anything to happen that God wouldn't have done anyway. This group would argue that our thoughts, beliefs, and actions are more of an aside because God will do what God will do, irrespective of what humans do.

But if God had really wanted to create a world where humans couldn't control things, then why did he create a world filled with laws—laws so specific and predictable that we can send a person to the moon and predict within a fraction of a second when he or she will land there? What if God created laws precisely so that we humans could have more control over our lives? The great apostle Paul wrote: "All things are yours, whether . . . the world or life or death or the present or the future—all are yours."[3] In another place he wrote, "Do not be deceived: God cannot be mocked. A man reaps what he sows."[4]

These texts assert that the way we participate in the world God created is much like how a farmer participates with the laws of nature. A farmer who wants the earth to yield a corn crop must learn to cooperate with nature to get it. Nature does not select the kind of harvest—it waits for the farmer to decide. The farmer makes that choice, actually predicting the field's future by the kind of seed that he sows there. To get a harvest of corn, the farmer simply plants corn seed.

I don't think God is the only one involved in determining how wonderful our lives are. In large part, *we* control the level of success we enjoy in our marriages, finances, careers, parenting, etc., based on whether we cooperate with the laws God put in place. We can have happiness or heartache, *on purpose*.

Believers in God often get mixed up on the balance between the things we are to do and the things God takes responsibility to do. If we're not careful, those of us who are God-followers will be guilty of something Jesus warned us about. In his parable of the talents, he urged people to work with the potential they had been given by God. But he indicated that some would be so oriented to the sovereignty of God that they would basically do nothing and resign themselves to fate. In other words, they'd join the Doris Day crowd, singing, "Que será, será, whatever will be, will be . . ." Jesus would say this bunch believes that God, like the master in his story, harvests what he has "not sown" and gathers where he has "not scattered seed." In other words, humans don't have to do jack— God does it all. People in this group bury their potential unproductively "in the ground"[5]—and this does not make God happy.

We are not subject to fate or sovereignty alone; we have something to say about how our lives turn out. Dr. Keith Bell said, "Persistence. Go for it. If you don't get it, give it another go. If that doesn't work, go again. If that still doesn't work, do it again; only with better preparation, more intensity, and greater passion. If that doesn't work, do it again only better. If that doesn't work, find another way. Stay with it. Pound away at it. Wear it down. Discover how to do it, but get it done."[6]

Make a conscious decision to invest your life rather than passively and fatalistically letting life "happen" to you. Even if you've been a consistent quitter, you can start turning that around today.

Developing Endurance

How do we do it? Where do we find the endurance necessary to win at life's tug-of-war? Here are four places to begin:

1. Life is full of possibilities; decide which ones fit you

This world is filled with so many possibilities that it can be disorienting—we find needs to be filled, problems to be solved, pain that cries out for relief, interests to explore, and so on. What we must understand is that people who succeed in life *make* things happen, while others *wait* for things to happen.

If you're going to sort through the possibilities being afforded to you by your unique blend of interests, talents, history, personality, and so on, you're going to need to take some time to pull away and do some meditative thinking. Your best shot at catching an accurate image of your face is when you gaze into a still

pond, not a rushing river. In times of quiet, uninter-
rupted silence, one's soul can grow still, and images appear more clearly. Once that occurs, you must decide
which possibilities will yield the best return for your
efforts.

If no direction seems obvious, start with simple
character development. This will make whatever path
you choose a rich adventure.

2. Decide what's most important

As you try to decide what possibilities you want to pursue, think through your values. What's most important
to you? Who is most important to you? What things can
you participate in that you will look back on later in life
and smile? What would you regret not doing? These
questions can lead you to a sense of personal mission—
what it is you feel you are here for.

I think personal mission is present in our lives before we notice what it is. Our mission touches our souls
and makes certain things more interesting to us than
others; it's the reason we cry over certain things and
laugh at the things we laugh about. It's the reason we
find some things fulfilling and others not; why some

places feel "right" to us while others don't. And though our personal mission is at play in our lives, we don't see it clearly until we pursue the clues for a while.

Ask yourself some good questions. Once the answers start to emerge, what's most important to you will begin to appear as well. When you begin pursuing goals that line up with your personal mission, endurance will fill your soul like a strong wind fills a sail. Energy will come effortlessly. Discover and focus on the things that give you inner happiness: those are the things that will fuel your success. Find the things that make you feel good, that resonate in your heart, and you will find the strength to endure.

3. Give voice to your dream

Talk may be cheap, but that's where all dreams start to take shape. Talk about what it is you want to do. But be careful about who you share your dreams with. Keep quiet until you find people who are both supportive and wise. Inspiration often comes as you dream out loud; when you give voice to your dreams, your thoughts will start to crystallize into plans. And as you talk about those plans, the places where your dreams need to be adjusted will become apparent too. *Plus*, making your dreams known to those you love will make you more accountable to those dreams.

4. Resist the temptation of sweet relief

Once upon a time, quitting was considered disgraceful. Today it's almost lauded. When you're under pressure, quitting really does feel like a wonderful wave of relief. But other waves follow: embarrassment, uncertainty about what's next, guilt, regret, and so on. Bill Hybels wrote:

> Watch the T.V. screen—things are tense at work. The employee is disagreeing with the boss. Nerves are snapping as the background music builds. The camera comes in tight on the employee and shows the veins popping out on his forehead. A moment of silence, and then his voice proclaims, "I quit!" The music crescendos wildly as he storms out, slamming the door behind him. And while the show's sponsors sing the praises of beer or antacids, viewers across the nation sigh and say, "That's exactly what I want to do to my boss someday. I want to quit in living

color, in front of a vast audience, with violins and a drum roll."

Look again—a husband and wife are disagreeing. The tension builds. At the peak of anger, the wife suddenly slaps her husband across the face, just as the cymbals crash, of course. Spinning on her heels, she storms out and slams the door just as the employee did on the last show. And half the wives in America say, "That's what I want to do. Johnny, get the pie tins and we'll go talk to Dad. This time I'm going to tell him to take a walk."

Watching these shows, we do not stop to think that the man is now unemployed, the woman is divorced and little Johnny doesn't have a dad anymore. All we see is the glamour, the sweet relief of cashing it in and walking out.[7]

Some things really are worth fighting for, even when they are deeply complicated or difficult. Make sure you consider what you would lose in quitting versus what you will enjoy if you keep hanging in there until things change.

Getting Unstuck

I think something in all of us believes life can be better. I don't think we're ever supposed to accept being stuck: stuck in dead relationships, stuck in destructive behavior patterns, stuck in poverty or a dead-end job, stuck in ill health, stuck in mental illness, stuck in anything. We may live in a world filled with hard places, but God is a redeemer—he will "provide a way out" when we find ourselves in hard places.[8] Change really is possible. But breaking out of "stuck" places and experiencing authentic change requires some work, some serious tugging—especially mental tugging.

The apostle Paul claimed that our lives are changed when we fight to think differently (biblically).[9] The ancient Hebrew proverb asserts, "As a man thinks in his heart, so is he."[10] In other words, you become what you think about the most. The universe is here because God thought of it. We are here because God thought of us. Because we are the only creatures in the world created in God's likeness, we, too, can think creatively—that is, we can participate in creative events.

Artists, architects, musicians, craftspeople, entrepreneurs, friends, lovers, everyday Joes and Janes, butchers, bakers, and candlestick makers—all of us get to be creative because we can think. Sure, we may not be able to create solar systems or make things out of nothing, but the creative capacity was placed in our souls by the Creator himself. And the whole process happens in the domain of thoughts.

This is why so much spiritual warfare surrounds a person's thought life. Scripture tells us that an enemy of our souls is trying to influence us with his evil imaginations. It declares, "Satan, who is the god of this world, has blinded the minds of those who don't believe."[11] Satan influences thought. Why? Because if he can influence our thoughts, then he can affect our lives.

God, on the other hand, calls us to take on *his* thoughts. "My thoughts are not your thoughts," he says in Isaiah 55:8, and he invites us to think as he thinks. This is why we are to give the Bible a place in our lives—it is God's Word, his thoughts. We are invited to take in God's thoughts so that we can step above our own limited thinking and begin to attract life of a higher order—eternal life, or the quality of life God himself enjoys. We are not just afforded peace; we are offered the peace of God. We are not just furnished joy; we can partake in the joy of the Lord. The apostle Peter wrote that by embracing the imaginings of God, we actually "participate in the divine nature."[12] It's all there for us, but not without some good old tug-of-war.

When you consider Satan's attempts to "blind" our minds versus God's call for us to adopt his thoughts, you have the makings of a knock-down, drag-out fight. But Paul wrote: "We use God's mighty weapons, not worldly weapons, to knock down the strongholds of human reasoning and to destroy false arguments. . . . We capture their rebellious thoughts and teach them to obey Christ."[13]

We are to do battle over which thoughts are permitted to dwell in our minds, because our thoughts matter. Our minds are not just passive holding zones, forced to think about whatever pops into them. We get to choose the thoughts we have, and we should fight hard, using the things God gives us to fight with for this fight. Paul wrote: "You'll do best by filling your minds and meditating on things true, noble, reputable, authentic, compelling, gracious—the best, not the worst; the beautiful, not the ugly; things to praise, not things to curse."[14]

Perhaps many of the problems in people's lives occur because people tend to dwell on bad stuff. Their chronic negative thinking keeps negative things chronically in their lives. When you focus on the negative, it stays. To have different experiences, you have to think different thoughts. The quote, "The significant problems we face cannot be solved at the same level of thinking we were at when we created them," is often attributed to Albert Einstein. Well said, Albert.

Most of us need a new level of thinking. We are used to looking on the negative side of things and have habitually practiced an expectation of dread. But when we persistently embrace godly thoughts, our lives will change!

The Good Life

Good marriages, sweet careers, and great communities don't just happen. They come as the result of persistence and determination. Don't be guilty of thinking that *hard* means "wrong," that if something requires sacrifice and some fighting, it's evidence that fate is against you. It's difficult to defend doing hard things, because ours is a society of hedonists. Hedonism is the belief that pleasure or happiness is the highest good. Hedonists are devoted to pleasure as a way of life. This is not to say that pleasure is evil; it's not. But making it your highest goal? Now that's a problem.

Sadly, our culture is not really open to anything as horrifyingly unpleasurable as discipline and commitment. We are way too self-indulgent. We believe the world is here for our own indulgence, and we feel we should be allowed to get away with doing whatever we want, whenever we want. But those who win in life are those who refuse to give in to "easy." They push past the quitting points and refuse to expect that everything will come to them instantly.

With a silly tug rope, my small dog Max illustrated what it takes to win in life—a flat-out refusal to quit. Refusing to quit will keep any human out of mediocrity and a passionless, vegetable-like life. You don't need to be an exceptionally talented, beautiful, or brilliant big dog to live large on this planet. Just refuse to quit, refuse to stop trying—hold on. Committing to the tug is huge—it's bigger than having talent, good looks, or smarts. Calvin Coolidge said, "Nothing in the world can take the place of persistence. Talent will not; nothing is more common than unsuccessful men with talent. Genius will not; unrewarded genius is almost a proverb. Education will not; the world is full of educated derelicts. Persistence and determination alone are omnipotent."[15] Even if you feel you are a lowbrow, frumpy, and ill-bred small dog, you can make up for it with persistence and determination.

You may be at a point where you feel like Bill, with the tractor on top of you. It doesn't matter—as long as you refuse to quit and are willing to fight, there's still hope. Decide never to give up. Take no prisoners. Lock into that tug, even if your feet aren't touching the ground and you're sure your teeth are going to be pulled out! God is so good that he will meet you where you are and turn your struggle into success.

Chapter 5

— ▬ ▬ ▬ ▬ ▬ —

Courage

F RANK IS A PRETTY OBEDIENT and compliant little dog. When you speak in a firm tone, his ears go down, he cowers a bit, and he obeys your command. But his willingness to comply does not mean he is cowardly. Quite the contrary. To my surprise, this dog has courage way beyond his size.

When Frank perceives anyone as a threat (kids playing too roughly, some big dude walking into the house, one of us lumbering in a playful, unfamiliar gait down the hall, etc.), he'll run at whoever it is with a you'd-better-back-off-now kind of bark. And he's unexpectedly intimidating. He's a courageous pup.

I think all of us love the idea of being courageous.

We don't relish the notion of being debilitated by fear or paralyzed by some overwhelming anxiety. We want to meet difficult challenges like the heroes we admire, not like cowards who cave in or compromise their values.

Ordinary Courage

When we think about a courageous person, we usually think of someone who does amazing things, like running into a burning building to save an elderly person or risking one's own life by jumping into floodwaters to save a mother and her baby—you know, things worthy of media coverage. But opportunities to perform those kinds of courageous acts are not afforded to most of us. And most of us secretly wonder whether we'd be brave enough or strong enough to pull off those acts if the situation arose.

But that doesn't mean that everyday people—the small dogs—can't have and display courage. We all face problems; we all have setbacks, troubles, and pain—such things are the stuff of life. Sadly, lots of folks don't set their sails to courageously face what life throws at them; they simply quit and end up getting towed.

Courage is an amazing thing because it helps us deal with whatever life throws at us—the good, the bad, and the ugly. And it helps us keep an even keel through it all. It emboldens us with fortitude to work through failure as well as helping us hold on to the personal integrity required to prevent compromise when we experience success. Courage helps us live well.

People of faith are at an advantage because, as Scripture tells us, "God did not give us a spirit of timidity, but a spirit of power."[1] Nice to know.

Three Types of Setback That Call for Courage

Life hands us three kinds of events or circumstances that require courage to face: ordinary life, life's bruises, and life's endings.

Ordinary Life

Someone once said to me, "The trouble with ordinary life is that it is so . . . *ordinary*." The ordinariness of life has a way of overwhelming us. The incessant to-do lists, e-mails, phone calls, appointments, errands, household chores, and relational responsibilities can be like the proverbial dripping faucet in our lives, threatening our sanity. It takes courage to face ordinary life because it is easier to run from daily responsibilities than to face them. Sometimes we run by jumping into innocuous things like watching too much TV or playing video games. Some want more thrill than TV affords, so they run to destructive things like illegal drug use or illicit sexuality.

At first blush it may be difficult to see the need for courage except when faced with extraordinary circumstances. But if you think about it, even the simple relational challenges we face day in and day out require a high level of courage.

Think about your relationship with God. Besides having to face the intellectual badgering you hear from the back row of atheists and agnostics, you have the dismissive so-you're-one-of-those-guys-who-needs-a-crutch judgments flying at you. It's scary to admit that you're a sinner. You have to admit that you've lied, hurt people, cheated, been greedy and self-centered, and so on. Lots of folks won't go there because they think it's too embarrassing. They lack courage. Not only does God call us to be honest with him; we need to be honest with one another—and that may be an even scarier enterprise. Committing to a daily relationship with God isn't for cowards and quiche eaters—it requires honesty, stamina, and plain old guts.

Or think about the courage necessary in something as ordinary as staying married to the same person your whole life. The idea of becoming one with another person is a cool idea, but there is plenty of *scary* involved. It's cool as long as you share similar attitudes and values and you bask in the warmth of agreement. But it gets scary and just plain awful when you run into things you clash over—then you really do want to run.

Or consider the courage it takes to raise children. Think of the issue of discipline alone. I was the dad who loved giving my kids whatever they wanted. But always giving children what they want is a recipe for raising third-world dictators, not responsible adults. Raising healthy, responsible adults requires doing an unfun, courageous thing: I had to learn to say no.

In the everyday of relationships, there are important admissions: "I'm sorry"; "That was my fault"; "I procrastinated and then completely forgot"; "This is who I am; I'm not happy about it, and I need help"; "I need to understand you better"—these are admissions that are required from time to time in healthy human interaction. But talk about scary . . .

It takes courage to not run from relational trouble. One of the laws of relationship is that tension demands attention. But most people are afraid to address and confront issues that need to be addressed and confronted. Avoidance is always easier than confrontation.

I remember when I was pastoring my first church and made a statement from the pulpit about someone's kids. I knew it was risky (they were in the audience), but I thought I had veiled my comment sufficiently. And, besides, I was right.

A couple of days went by, and I got a letter from the mom. It kindly asked why I would refer to her family in a public forum and wondered if they should leave the church. The letter was stained with tears.

I felt trapped. Part of me screamed, *She's overreacting. I was just making a point!* Another part of me whispered, *You shouldn't have done that. Go and ask them to forgive you.* That whisper paralyzed me with fear. But against the gravitational pull of fright, I got up from my desk, went to my car, drove to their home in complete dread that they might actually be there (it was a Saturday morning), walked up to the door, and knocked. They answered. I stayed for an hour or so explaining what I was thinking—while still owning my mistake—and asking them to forgive me for being insensitive. They were gracious enough to do so.

I learned something important about courage that day. Courage is not the absence of fear; it's doing what's right in spite of fear. Don't think that if you're riddled with fear courage has somehow evaded you. Look straight into that fear, focus on what's right, and then do it—afraid. That's what courage is. John Wayne once said, "Courage is being scared to death, but saddling up anyway."[2]

Just because things get difficult and uncomfortable doesn't mean you should avoid them. Decades ago W. Beran Wolfe wrote: "If you have evaded all unpleasantness in your life your happiness is placed in unstable equilibrium by the constant dread that some unavoidable disappointment is just around the corner. If you have faced pain and disappointment, you not only value your happiness more highly, but you are prepared for [the] unpredictable. There may be many happy human vegetables who have succeeded in avoiding unhappiness and pain, but they cannot call themselves human."[3]

So much of the good stuff can only be had after you've walked through the land of hard. Norman Vincent Peale said, "Too much caution is bad for you. It is usually wiser to stand up to a scary-seeming experience and walk right into it, risking the bruises or hard knocks. You are likely to find it is not as tough as you had thought. Or you may find it plenty tough, but also discover you have what it takes to handle it."[4]

Instead of avoiding something that makes you feel bad or scared, ponder whether it's good. Look into the future. What would your life be like if you continued with that course of action? Would it be good? Would your life be richer? If you determine that it's something good (though the thought of trying it makes you feel afraid now), decide to start thinking about it differently—refuse to play it safe. I have heard it said, "A ship in harbor is safe—but that is not what ships are for." You were not created for "safe" either.

Look past the pain of the action to the joy of its reward. Then do the uncomfortable, hard thing courageously, and do it with joy. Rejigger your emotions and commit to the thing; don't let your feelings set the course of your life. If you let your emotions rule you, there's a chance you may end up ruining a lot of things that could have been wonderful.

Life's Bruises

We don't just need courage to face ordinary life; we need courage to face the places in our lives where we have been emotionally and psychologically broken.

Everyone on this planet comes from the land of broken toys.

Some issues in our lives are beyond a quick fix. Feelings of emptiness and fear usually have deep roots, as do feelings of inferiority or shame—these have a certain level of complexity to them. And we often don't understand why we're feeling the way we are. Sometimes our brokenness can be traced to a tragic moment in childhood. Other times feelings of dread may lurk in the back of our psyches because of a past offense or personal failure—then, whenever we get into a situation remotely similar to the one where we failed (or were abused), we instantly start to feel all those bad feelings again, often without consciously knowing why.

What do we do with these toxic emotions? Some choose to play the role of victim. The tragedy of accepting that role is that you have to buy into the idea that whatever happens to you has the right to govern who you ultimately become. This kind of resignation and passivity usually leads to despair. In this view, the only way to change one's life is to change the past or to change the whole world first—and that's not going to happen.

We can only progress in life when we are willing to take responsibility for our own actions and attitudes no matter what has happened to us. I like Laura Schless-inger's no-nonsense take on this: "I don't believe for a minute that everything that happens to you is your doing or your fault. But I do believe the ultimate quality of your life and your happiness is determined by your courageous and ethical choices and your overall attitude. You may get shipped some bad bricks and weak steel, but you are still the general contractor."[5]

It takes courage to not play the blame game and to refuse the epithet *victim*.

The other path people take when dealing with their feelings of brokenness is to simply try to ignore them, pretending all is well (Christians are notorious for this). But it doesn't work. Ignoring your brokenness produces crippling and chronically painful emotions. The only way to keep negative emotions from controlling us is by becoming radically honest—and that definitely takes courage. God does not want his children living in brokenness, and he promises to heal us; but that doesn't mean it's easy to experience healing.

Bottom line, we will never get anywhere near freedom if we keep pretending all is well when it is not. We're not supposed to try to trick our minds into believing we live in Wonderland when we're really camping right outside the gates of hell. Wholeness is enjoyed as we take God by the hand and let him lead us on the precarious path of appropriately dealing with the past and joyfully facing the future. God is the one who gives us tools that "have divine power to demolish strongholds."[6]

Those of us who follow Jesus practice living by faith, which means we often ignore our feelings as we trust the Lord. But ignoring our feelings has nothing to do with faith if those feelings are evidence of an inner brokenness. In fact, ignoring those kinds of feelings will keep us from being radically transformed by God.

In his book *Emotionally Healthy Spirituality*, Peter Scazzero does a brilliant job discussing the average Christian's aversion to feelings that evidence their brokenness and how that often leads to unresolved anger and frustration. Scazzero claims that many believers are difficult to be around because they have not learned how to process the brokenness deep within them. Instead of going to God with our bad feelings and emotions, Scazzero says believers actually use God to run from God. He explains: "On the surface all appears to be healthy and working, but it's not. All those hours and hours spent lost in one Christian book after another . . . all those many Christian responsibilities outside the home or going from one seminar to another . . . all that extra time in prayer and Bible study. . . . At times we use these Christian activities as an unconscious attempt to escape from pain."[7]

Here's a wild thought: what if God actually created us to experience bad feelings so we could have a built-in indicator of our inner brokenness? We know we were created with physical nerves that warn us through pain—that's how we know when we step on a nail or have an infection. Why would God do such a thing, you might ask. Maybe so we can address the problem and experience healing. If that were true, it sure would cause us to rethink the bad feelings we encounter. Instead of trying to deny them or run from them, we would be encouraged to follow them back to their source with the hope that God would meet us with healing.

Scazzero wrote:

Many of us Christians believe wholeheartedly that anger, sadness, and fear are sins to be avoided, indicating something is wrong with our spiritual life. Anger is dangerous and unloving toward others. Sadness indicates a lack of faith in the promises of God; depression surely reveals a life outside the will of God! And fear? The Bible is filled with commands to "not be anxious about anything" and "do not fear" (see Philippians 4:6 and Isaiah 41:10).

So what do we do? We try to inflate our-

selves with a false confidence to make those
feelings go away. We quote Scripture, pray
Scripture, and memorize Scripture—anything
to keep ourselves from being overwhelmed by
those feelings![8]

Feelings, he argues, are often affected by the sinis-
ter voices from our surrounding world and our broken
pasts. They haunt us with deeply held negative beliefs
that make us feel:

I am a mistake.
I am a burden.
I am stupid.
I am worthless.
I must be approved of by certain people in order to
   be okay.
I don't have the right to experience joy and plea-
   sure.
I don't have the right to assert myself and say what I
   think and feel.
I don't have the right to feel good about myself.[9]

Scazzero asserts that we must not bury these feelings but rather unearth them in God's presence. He
says we cannot really listen to what God is saying or

evaluate what's going on in our lives if we ignore the negative emotions. We need to process our feelings, never ignore or suppress them.

For example: The Bible commands us to love those around us, but there's this guy you sort of love to hate. You refuse to keep fueling your unloving feelings—not by denying those feelings but by processing them. You ask God to help you understand why you have feelings of hatred; why this deep brokenness is in you to begin with. Perhaps the guy reminds you of someone who hurt you in the past. You ask God to help you forgive and to appreciate and love him as God does. At first it feels like it's killing you, but you continue to trust God's hand in your soul to work through the forgiveness and to process your feelings enough that you actually begin to feel love for the guy. The Bible calls this kind of feeling reorientation getting your "senses trained,"[10] and it is the stuff of transformation.

Here's a brainteaser: maybe we should feel good about feeling bad. Why? Because pain is a gift—it points us to the place where "unwholeness" lies—to damaged places in our souls that need repair.

When I go to my doctor with an ache or pain, he asks me, "Where does it hurt?" When I tell him my symptoms, he can diagnose what's going on and recommend a course of action. Pain was the gift that revealed that there was trouble in my body—it was my signal to get some repair. The pain was never really the problem, the problem was the problem—the pain just alerted me to the problem—it brought it to my attention.

Dr. Paul Brand is famous for his work among lepers. Leprosy is one of those diseases people don't like to talk about. That's because when it goes untreated, the patients suffer horrible disfigurement: their noses shrink away; they lose fingers and toes, then hands and feet. Many go blind.

In his work with lepers, Dr. Brand discovered that it was not the disease that caused patient's flesh to deteriorate—at least not directly. Their disfigurement was actually the result of their not feeling pain. Lepers, it turns out, destroy themselves unwittingly. They step on pieces of glass and don't feel it. They break a toe or scrape off their skin and flesh down to the bone without so much as a twinge of pain.

Brace yourself. This next part is pretty graphic.

One day Dr. Brand arrived at one of the leprosariums in India to conduct a group clinic. His visit had been announced in advance, and when the administrators of the camp rang the bell to get patients' attention, a large group of lepers quickly began to move to the area where the clinic was to be held.

Dr. Brand noticed one patient emerging from the crowd, trying to beat the rest of them to the tent. At first the young man struggled across the edge of the courtyard with his crutches, holding his bandaged left leg clear of the ground. But as some other patients began to get ahead of him, he decided to race. As Dr. Brand watched, this guy tucked his crutches under his arm and began running. He ended up near the head of the line, where he stood panting, leaning on his crutches, and sporting a huge smile of triumph.

Dr. Brand knew from the odd way he'd run that something was seriously wrong. Walking toward the patient to investigate, he saw that the man's bandages were wet with blood, and his left foot flopped freely from side to side. By running on an already dislocated ankle, he had put far too much force on the end of his leg bone and had ripped away the flesh under the stress. He had no clue that he was running on the end of his tibia bone. As Dr. Brand knelt beside him, he found that small stones and twigs had jammed through the end of the bone into the marrow cavity. He had no choice but to amputate the leg just below the knee.[11]

Okay. Horrible story. But I had to tell it to drive home this one point: pain is a gift. True, it's a gift most people don't want. But if we try to avoid pain, we're really setting ourselves up for emotional leprosy, not personal transformation. Bad feelings can reveal secrets about our brokenness and about how that brokenness has influenced what we now believe about our lives. Don't run through life avoiding your emotional pain. You'll just jam more negative sticks and stones into the marrow of your soul. Locate your bad feelings. Take them to God. Ask him for the courage to see what those feelings are indicating, and let him heal you.

Life's Endings

At times in life, something happens that is beyond repair—the loss of a loved one, the aftermath of a violent crime or crippling accident, a horrible divorce, a debilitating illness or handicap, and the like. Facing and processing endings without caving in to self-pity and bitterness of soul requires courage on steroids.

But the ending that requires courage at its best is the end of life. Death requires the unique courage of letting go of life and committing to the unknown. Luke recorded Jesus' facing this ending with courage: "Jesus called out with a loud voice, 'Father, into your hands I commit my spirit.' When he had said this, he breathed his last."[12]

Most folks are scared to death about death, so they live in denial of it. Those outside the faith tend to hope technology will conquer death before they face it; those in the church hope Jesus comes and they'll fly away without having to deal with it. Few actually face the fact that the odds are they're going to die—and not all that far in the future.

The psalmist prayed: "Teach us to number our days aright."[13] This prayer shows that we are supposed to think about death as a motivator to live well before we face God. But most of us don't have the courage to face death head on—too creepy. The writer of the book of Hebrews claimed that for most people, "all their lives were held in slavery by their fear of death."[14]

I think this is a significant way we small barking dogs can stand out. We need to have courage about death. We are people of faith; we should think differently about death than unbelievers do. Read how the apostle Paul showed no fear of death: "I trust that my life will bring honor to Christ, whether I live or die. For to me, living means living for Christ, and dying is even better. But if I live, I can do more fruitful work for Christ. So I really don't know which is better. I'm torn between two desires: I long to go and be with Christ, which would be far better for me. But for your sakes, it is better that I continue to live."[15]

The tone of Paul's perspective is that those who are living for Christ and not for themselves get to live here until they are done here—until they have completed their mission. This offers great security to Christ-followers. It suggests they will not die until they are ready to die. Somehow a person bent on following God's path is assured freedom from accidental death.

It's sort of reminiscent of the movie *The Blues Brothers*, where brothers Jake (played by John Belushi) and Elwood (played by Dan Aykroyd) team up to raise money for a Catholic charity by getting their old blues band together. On their journey they get into destructive car chases; are involved in an apartment-building explosion; have a flamethrower fired at them while they're in a telephone booth, which blows up a nearby propane tank; and have an automatic weapon shot at them. But they emerge from it all unscathed because they are "on a mission from God."

So are we.

I have a friend named Keith Wheeler who carries a cross around the world. He started carrying his twelve-foot wooden cross on Good Friday back in 1985. He has since carried that cross over nineteen thousand miles through more than 185 countries on all seven continents. He's been to Tibet, Iran, Iraq, China, and even Antarctica. He has walked through the Middle East, North Africa, and many former Iron Curtain countries—before the political changes. Keith has carried his cross through many nations at war, such as Bosnia, Rwanda, and Chechnya, and in Bethlehem during the standoff at the Church of the Nativity. During this time he has been arrested many times (never for crimes) and even jailed.

Keith has shared harrowing stories with me about meeting wild animals, poisonous insects, killer snakes, and wild humans. Once he was taken before a firing squad to be shot; another time he was beaten and left for dead.

One day I asked him, "Does the idea of dying ever freak you out?"

"Not really," he said in his kind, thoughtful way. "I figure my life is in God's hands as long as I'm doing what he has asked me to do. I'll go after I'm finished with my mission on this planet. My death won't be an accident."

The guy's a Blues Brother at heart (his courage puts even Frank to shame).

A number of letters have been discovered that were written by Christian martyrs during the first three centuries that show great courage in the face of death. One saint wrote: "In a dark hole I have found cheerfulness; in a place of bitterness and death I have found rest. While others weep I have found laughter, where others fear I have found strength. Who would believe that in a state of misery I have had great pleasure; that in a lonely corner I have had glorious company and in the hardest of bonds perfect repose. All those things Jesus has granted me. He is with me, comforts me and fills me with joy. He drives bitterness from me and fills me with strength and consolation."[16]

This is courage to the end.

William Shakespeare wrote:

Cowards die many times before their deaths;
The valiant never taste of death but once.
Of all the wonders that I yet have heard,
It seems to me most strange that men should fear;
Seeing that death, a necessary end,
Will come when it will come.[17]

Courageous Prayer

Little dogs can have the kind of courage that helps them face the daily noise of life; the kind that helps them be

honest as they face their own brokenness and the healing that can ensue; and the courage that helps them
accept what they cannot change. We need wisdom to
discern the differences in the challenges. That reminds
me of the famous prayer attributed to Dr. Reinhold
Niebuhr: "God, give us the grace to accept with serenity the things that cannot be changed, courage to change
the things which should be changed, and the wisdom to
distinguish the one from the other."[18]

The opportunities to be courageous pop up all
around us every day—from facing today's to-do list, to
confronting the people who are trying to con or use us,
to using common sense when the tide of popular opin-
ion makes no sense at all. Courage is needed in our lives
from beginning to end.

When it comes to courage, big dogs have no advantage over small ones. Size is irrelevant. Having the bark
of courage will make you stand out and enable you to
live large. And remember, having courage doesn't mean
you're not scared out of your wits; it just means doing
what's right in spite of being afraid.

The famous World War II general George S. Patton Jr. said, "If we take the generally accepted definition
of bravery as a quality which knows no fear, I have
never seen a brave man. All men are frightened. The

more intelligent they are, the more frightened they are. The courageous man is the man who forces himself, in spite of his fears, to carry on."[19]

Courageous people cannot be ignored—no matter how small they are.

Chapter 6

The Bark of Faith

I LIKE SMALL DOGS BEST. I know they don't stand out like the big dogs. The only big dog that ever lived with Gail and me was a Great Dane named Katy. She stood out, all right—she was enormous. She really belonged to my mom, but after the vet told her Katy was going to die, I offered to take her in for a while to care for her and to pray for her to get healthy again. I wasn't sure it would happen, but I figured it was worth a shot.

We took care of Katy for about six weeks and, to our surprise, she recovered completely. But I never really "got" Katy. Even after she was healthy, she just didn't seem to have all that much personality.

Frank, on the other hand, is all jacked up with personality. And when you observe him, he comes across like a genius at life. He leads the closest I've seen to a stress-free existence. Aside from his predictable frenzy in alerting us to the presence of a stranger at the front door, his earnestness about the need for a potty break, and the agonizing anticipation of feeding time, he shows no real signs of tension or unhappiness. He certainly has no problem getting enough sleep (this dog has mastered the Sabbath). No matter what life delivers, Frank throws himself into it. And he's a blast to watch. Whether it's front-door guard duty, eating, sleeping, going outside, or playing, he is fully present in the moment.

Small dogs do stand out—they just don't do it the same way big dogs do. I've been trying to make the case that although you may see yourself as a small dog in this big-dog world—you're just a mom or a dockworker or a plumber or a nurse or a Starbucks manager—you can still stand out in ways that change the world. You may not have all the power and authority and status the big dogs have, but that doesn't mean you can't have a bark that simply can't be ignored or that you can't stand out in the small-dog way.

I think the single most significant way we can stand out in this world is through our bark of faith. I'm not talking about spiritually blathering or bullhorning people about faith; I'm talking about living a life of faith that "barks." St. Francis of Assisi is credited with saying: "Preach the gospel always. If necessary, use words." That holds true here.

Yet faith is a gnarly adventure. Besides the obvious—God is invisible, and how does one connect with someone who's invisible?—faith is also a tad mystical. But before we get to that, let's talk about how your faith perspective contextualizes life in a way that impacts everything: the way you live, the goals you set, the way you handle your money, how you approach human relationships, the entertainment you take in—everything. Faith starts when you buy into a unique story. What you think the story is—your take on what's going on around you—influences your approach to life. So what in the world *is* going on? What's your take? What is the metanarrative—the story behind the events we see going on in the world?

Three Defining Stories of Existence

J. R. R. Tolkien's Middle-earth saga *Lord of the Rings* features a fantasy world filled with all kinds of beings: Men, Hobbits, Elves, Dwarves, Dragons, Orcs, and

Trolls, and the lesser-known Balrogs, Nazgûls, Ents, and Woses. All of these races had differing histories, beliefs, credos, cultures, ethical codes, and legends—how they interpreted reality varied; their stories varied. And the stories they believed shaped the lives they lived.

Philosophically, people in Western society today are as divergent in their beliefs and interpretations of daily events as the creatures from Tolkien's Middle-earth. The apostle Paul warned about this. He said we live in a world of contrasting stories and interpretations. He said those holding differing points of view would always try to squeeze us into agreeing with them. Each alternate story claimed certain things about God (or the gods), about the role of the human race (who we are), and about what the future holds. Paul challenged the church not to "conform" into believing stories concocted by people.[1] He claimed that the Scriptures tell us the story from God's point of view and that if we would listen to and embrace that story, our lives would be "transformed."[2] What are some of these ways of viewing life?

The Biblical Story

At the risk of sounding overly simplistic, here's the short version of the biblical story: Reality as we know it is the result of a God who created everything we see. Yet he is not limited by what he made—he lives both inside and outside of creation. He created the world because he wanted to be a part of it—to pour his life into it. As part of a means to this end, he created a race of beings that would be able to represent his wisdom and care within creation. And he created them to be a little different from everything else here, to be bearers of something unique: he breathed into us (not into any other creature) his very breath.[3] His breath in human life was the chief way God was entering his creation. He wanted his glory to be present in this world through the human experience.

But in tragic irony, the very beings God created so that he might have access into the world rebelled against his intention; we lost our way. And we lost access to his breath—his presence. We died spiritually, and creation was alienated from its creator.[4] The good news is that God is not just a creator; he is a redeemer—a restorer. And in a completely appropriate way, God resolved the problem by finding a way to reconnect with the human race. Jesus Christ came to this planet (entered the limitations of creation) to take on our spiritual death, and he found a way to "re-breath" us—to cause us to be, in a spiritual sense, "born again."[5] Now God's breath is back. He again indwells his human creatures and ultimately will do so with all of creation (see Revelation 21 and 22). He will transform creation into what it was made for from the beginning—a habitation for God and his children.

This biblical God-story is completely subversive to every other one being told in our day—and there are many. Let's look at a couple.

A Popular Modern Story: Life Is a Roll of the Dice

One of the most popular stories in modern times is the one that says life is the product of random chance—that random events gave birth to the universe. Believing this, that the universe is here by chance and that we simply happened into it, is a decidedly different position from believing in a God who made it all. If there is no God or any intelligent design, reality becomes arbitrary—it's whatever you want to be, whatever you want to call it. If this is the case, there is no universal basis for meaning, for morality, or for human identity. History is irrelevant—the sequence of events have no meaning, no reason for what happens. Everything is random. If one accepts this story, the stage is set for the apostles of absurdity to convince anyone of anything—for then all beliefs, ideas, and creeds are equally valid. After all, this is a dice-tossed world.

Buying into the story that life is random shapes your life in significant ways. It forces you to view the universe as purposeless and cold. In such a world, there is no need for prayer except for something like the verses of an old Stephen Crane poem from the 1800s:

A man said to the universe:
"Sir, I exist!"
"However," replied the universe,
"The fact has not created in me
A sense of obligation."[6]

In this story there is no creation; things have always just been here. There are no miracles. Matter exists, and nothing else is of any consequence. The astrophysicist Carl Sagan (in mocking liturgical tone), summarizes this story well: "The Cosmos is all that is or ever was or ever will be."[7]

Who you are, according to this view, is no one in particular. We are not special or chosen. We arrived here because our number came up, like a number in a Las Vegas game. Our only hope for standing out is our own self-actualization—the pursuit of excellence through our actions, achievements, aspirations, and capacities; mitigated, of course, by our stupid failures and obvious limitations. But there's no such thing as destiny. No one is looking out for us or planning anything for us. Human beings are just complex machines that have personality because of chemical and physical interactions we do not fully understand. The mystery of life is not genuine mystery; it is mechanical complexity. Death is not a transition from one kind of living to another; it's simply the extinction of personality and individuality.

The upside of believing everything is here by chance is that you don't have to blame anyone for the parts of your life that suck. But the downside is the necessary conclusion that nothing has any purpose, that life is absurd and pointless. Jean-Paul Sartre, one storyteller of the "chance" view, wrote: "Every existing thing is born without reason, prolongs itself out of weakness, and dies by chance. I leaned back and closed my eyes. . . . I knew it was the World, the naked World suddenly revealing itself, and I choked with rage at this gross absurd being."[8] Obviously not Hallmark-card material, but it is telling and points to where the "dice-tossed world" story ultimately lands.

A Variation That Includes God and Chance

Another variation of the "chance" story accepts the notion that God may have created everything that exists but holds that he no longer has anything more to do with it. God is seen as a cosmic clockmaker who leaves his creation to run on it's own. The universe is the giant clock whose gears and levers mesh with mechanical precision, ticktocking through time in a perfectly ordered way—all on its own. God is not present. He is not personal. And there is no Big Plan. God is distant and unknowable, living well outside the affairs of the world, which cannot and do not touch him.

If you buy into this story wholesale, there's a fairly good chance that the shape or order of your life is characterized by a kind of me-first, I'm-going-to-grab-all-the-marbles-I-can gusto. After all, God is indifferent and is not looking out for you. You have to fend for yourself.

The Importance of Story

The story you believe will profoundly impact the way you feel about yourself and how you respond to the things that happen to you. Embracing the God-story is subversive because it means that almighty God longs to be engaged in our human lives. That means we don't have to face the vicissitudes of life alone or deal with stuff from our own limited, finite perspective. Having God's help with life's issues is huge—it would be like paying your monthly bills from a checking account shared with Bill Gates. Takes a lot of the sweat out.

One of the Bible writers said it this way: "God has said, 'Never will I leave you; never will I forsake you.' So we say with confidence, 'The Lord is my helper; I will not be afraid.'"[9] Another one said: "If God is for us, who can be against us? . . . We are more than conquerors through him who loved us."[10]

Living a life of faith—actually believing in the divine connection—will make you stand out. Such a life gives even small dogs a significant bark that cannot be ignored. Paul described the impact we can have in a faithless world as shining "like stars in the universe."[11] But having faith is more than just believing a story. Faith has a deep level of divine mystery to it. It isn't just you loving God on your own. The real importance of faith is not what we do for God or believe about him but what we do *with* him. Faith isn't as much about a belief in God as it is about a relationship with him.

The Bible is full of examples of men and women

who demonstrated their faith through their relationship with God. And those who had this relationship were those who most desired it and sought out God's presence. When God told Moses to go into the wilderness, Moses replied: "If your Presence does not go with us, do not send us up from here."[12] When Jesus commissioned his followers to "Go and make disciples," the most valuable thing he could give them was his presence: "And surely I am with you always, to the very end of the age."[13] Christian spirituality is not about what we do apart from God.

God's presence in our lives—our relationship with him—is what gives us the bark of faith the world cannot ignore. But we must be careful not to let the vibrancy of that relationship fade over time to a mere shadow or form—to where we are going through the motions of relationship with God but without the emotion of a real spiritual connection. The Bible gives some examples of people like this too. In a vision given to the apostle John, recorded in the book of Revelation, Jesus addressed his followers in the church of Ephesus. These folks had been apprentices of Jesus for a while. And they were doing pretty well in some things. Jesus commended them for their hard work and perseverance. He applauded them for refusing to tolerate false teachers and wicked people. He acknowledged the hardships they had suffered for his name without growing weary. But then he said: "Yet I hold this against you: You have forsaken your first love."[14]

Obviously, these people loved God. They loved him enough to persevere for him in spite of difficulties: they had a devoted love. They loved him enough to protect the integrity of his message: they had a rational, intellectual love. They displayed a love willing to lose and accept hardship for God: they had a sacrificial love. They had a committed love that refused to grow weary. But they had forsaken the intensity of their first love. And Jesus wasn't happy. In fact, he said that if they didn't correct the situation, they would lose their capacity to represent him effectively in the world: "I will come to you and remove your lampstand from its place."[15]

The problem was, though they loved Jesus in a number of ways, they no longer had a longing for the presence of God himself.

Faith is more than maintaining doctrinal purity. That's good, but it isn't enough.

Faith is more than maintaining separation from the world and from sin. That's good, but it isn't enough either.

Faith is more than daily devotions, following God's laws, and volunteering in church—all those things are good, but they are not enough.

Those things can be done without the direct presence of God. They are not "otherly" enough.

Jesus calls this "otherly" love "first love." Those of us who have fallen in love remember first-love feelings. The ones we loved captured our attention. Thoughts of them filled our minds. We eagerly anticipated their presence. We longed to be with them. It was definitely "otherly." Later we matured into devoted love, rational love, intellectual love, and sacrificial love. But those kinds of love can be present in us when the one being loved is absent. First love fights for the presence of the one who is loved.

I think Jesus wants us to remember that faith is mostly about longing to be with Another. At its core, faith is not a commitment to fulfilling religious duty but to connecting with the person of God himself. We need to find God in prayer. We need to find him at church. Finding God should be our focus when we skip a meal or retreat into a season of silence. We need to be like the psalmist who wrote, "My whole being follows hard after You and clings closely to You."[16] We also need to be like Moses, who said, "Unless you go with us, we don't want to go."[17]

It's easy to make faith religious or philosophical or intellectual or into some kind of inane belief. It only gets real and gritty when you pull aside into a secret, quiet place and lift your hands or get on your knees or lie on your face and begin to call out to God—to chase after him. It gets real when you skip a meal and, as the hunger pangs grip you, say: "I'm hungry for you, God. My body is screaming for a Big Mac and fries. I can almost taste them. But I'm more hungry for you than for physical food."

This makes faith more than a set of principles, a doctrine, a code of conduct, a self-discipline, service to God and others, integrity, or even a personal commitment. These can be done quite humanly and independent of the actual presence of God. In the real presence of God, things change. You think differently. You forgive more easily. You are more gracious, less self-pitying. You have been with Another, and you are "otherly" in your demeanor.

Sadly, many of us assume that the primary source of spirituality, meaning, and value lies in our own minds— how we think about God and revere him in our own understanding. But the saints who went before us traced it back to deeper ground. They saw it as transcendent, or beyond the believer. It is bigger than us. God is in the mix of faith. Faith is about being captured by a transcendent, bigger-than-us, "otherly" experience with the living God. It is precisely this "otherliness," this transcendent connection, that makes loving God so rich.

Being with God

Christian spirituality is the result of God's indwelling the human soul. Paul wrote: "Do you not know that your body is a temple of the Holy Spirit, who is in you, whom you have received from God?"[18] Christian theism holds that when a person crosses the threshold of faith, God unites himself to that person on the level of being.

This is a little difficult to explain, so bear with me.

Only God can unite himself to another on the level of being. When we think of uniting with others, we think of joining ourselves with them through interactions like conversation or by doing some activity together (one sings bass, another tenor, and we join together in song), or we have a meeting of the minds on a particular subject—this is the human sense of joining.

When God joins himself to you, however, the things you do proceed from both God and you (as long as your heart is submitted to his presence). We're talking here about a joining on the level of persons. God and you are united and act out as persons together. This is the mystery of faith.

A faith action is not a blend of God and you operating; it is both of you acting together as one—in one sense, it is fully human and fully divine. The act belongs to you, and it belongs to God. It is both God's action and your action at the same time. For example, you come home from work exhausted. You face your family and sense a nudge inside from God to smile and take some interest in your family. You feel the inclination to smile (by virtue of God speaking it to you, it has already become your own inclination), and you either follow it or sink back into your own tiredness. If you don't engage, the inclination of faith is aborted. But if you do engage, it is a faith-filled self-expression that is literally both human and divine. It is your personal act of self-expression, but you and God are united on the same level of person, expressing one and the same act of love in one act of caring.

To grow in spirituality means you must grow in deeper union with God on a personal level. It means you have to cultivate more awareness of the impulses of God's person within your heart while becoming less and less resistant to those impulses. It means that when you think of your human person or self, you associate less and less with the idea of the isolated human self and more and more with being joined with God. This is how you can say along with Paul, "I no longer live, but Christ lives in me."[19] It isn't that you lose yourself, but that you discover your true self in Christ. Jesus Christ is no longer the "other" who speaks to you; his voice becomes your voice as you surrender to him.

When you figure out how to live like this in a world

that is not used to matters of faith, you stand out. You'll be barking, baby. Whether you're a maid, a construction worker, a file clerk, a medical doctor, or an Avon lady, if you are filled with a robust faith, you will stand out in front of those you come in contact with. It is impossible not to.

Toxic Faith

We need to fight to keep faith pure. Faith gets toxic when we make it too human centered. What do we do that makes it too centered on us?

Trying to Impress Others

Trying to impress others is always a losing proposition. I think we sometimes fall prey to making faith less about pleasing God and more about trying to impress and please other people. We want to belong (to not belong brings terror), so it's pretty easy to concentrate on meeting the expectations of others in the hopes that we'll be able to belong. The problem is that others want us to look exactly like them; they expect us to give up our own distinctiveness.

Paul wrote that we are all different, like the parts of the human body, and he challenged each member to dare to be different—not to act and think the exact same way.[20] Yes, we are all supposed to be holy. Yes, we are all supposed to be moral. Yes, we are all supposed to live ethically. But we are each to live out our holiness in the way we are wired—in a manner guided by our unique gifts, passions, and personalities. Some of us may be more fashionable than others, some more conservative, others more edgy. Some of us are quiet, others bombastic. Some are tattoo friendly, others tattoo phobic.

The apostle Paul said: "I have become all things to all men so that by all possible means I might save some."[21] Maybe as we all express ourselves in ways that are congruent with our talents, passions, and personalities, we are best positioned to "save some"—because those "some" can relate to us as we truly are.

Christianity is not supposed to be a retread of Eastern mysticism that forces people to forfeit their distinctiveness as they are absorbed into some great cosmic oneness or sameness. But sameness makes it easier for us to identify the insiders. Just as black leather and a Harley-Davidson are the marks of a biker; and blue jeans, western boots, and a huge silver belt buckle are the marks of a cowboy, certain external attributes are

fancied by some Christians as the marks of Christlike-
ness. It's easy to make Christianity about externals and
man-made rules. But the downside is, unless you already fit the predetermined collection of personality
traits set by the Christian culture to which you belong,
you'll have to become something you're not. Christianity will likely feel restrictive and hold little joy for you.
Satan loves that. He wants us all confused about what
real Christianity is so that we'll live in some kind of
powerless, synthetic belief system.

Focusing on Achievement

Faith gets toxic when we make it about achievement. I
don't know why so many of us shift the footing of our
faith from trusting God and what he does in our lives
to trying to ramp up our own achievements and trusting that. It doesn't make sense to trust ourselves. The
whole faith thing started with God. Faith itself is a gift.[22]
Though a changed life (a great achievement) is always
the result when a person relies on Jesus, Christianity
isn't about human achievement.

Faith and discipleship were never supposed to be
centered on a person committing to do good; they're to
be about committing to God—the one who does good

things *in* us. We can't produce Christianity. It's super-natural. A promise at the altar to be good means about as much to God as promising to fly for him. He knows we can't fly.

Only Superman can fly.

In the arena of faith, only the God-man, Jesus, can fly. People can't. Humans will never be able to pull off divine goodness. That stuff is from another world. True, if you get up real high (really, really, really try to live right) and jump, you'll have the illusion of flight, but it won't end well.

Walking by faith is not about learning how to fly. Faith is about staying connected with Jesus, the only real Superman who ever lived. We must fight to keep faith from becoming about our own achievement, or it will turn toxic.

Thinking We Can Earn God's Love

Faith also gets toxic when we try to earn God's love. Trust me, you don't want what you have truly earned from God. Far better than that, faith is about being credited with what Jesus earned for us by his actions.

God's love for us is an amazing thing. It makes no sense at all. God lovingly chases us when we are completely unworthy of that love. When the psalmist caught a glimpse of the love and favor God had for him, he cried, "This is too much, too wonderful—I can't take it all in!"[23] Neither can we. God's love may resemble the natural kindness and love families and married couples share, but it goes far deeper, is completely unconditional, and will never die.

I totally get how some people think all this is too good to be true. How *can* it be true? How can God be so reckless about giving to us when we're so good at being so bad? But that is exactly what he's like. We matter to him, and there's nothing we can do to alter that. Paul prayed for his friends: "May you have the power to understand, as all God's people should, how wide, how long, how high, and how deep his love is."[24] It takes power to understand God's love and grace toward us— God has to help us see it.

The truth is, we're not all that good. In fact, what we seem to do best is botch things up. God forgives us; we fail again. God gives us courage; we get discouraged. God gives us a dream; we make it a self-actualizing quest filled more with us than with God. God gives us gifts; we go prodigal with them and use them for our own advantage. Let's face it: if we were God, we would probably kill us.

The wonderful news is that God knows us completely *and still loves us*. J. I. Packer wrote: "There is tre-mendous relief in knowing that his love to me is utterly realistic, based at every point on prior knowledge of the worst about me, so that no discovery now can disillu-sion him about me, in the way I am so often disillu-sioned about myself."[25]

God bases his decision to pursue us and work in us on his unconditional love. Unconditional love loves without stipulation or requirement—it isn't based on the actions of the one being loved. This God kind of love simply imparts value to us. We are precious to God. It isn't earned; it just *is*. We are loved because we are. We belong because we are. When this truth be-comes real to us, we no longer fear abandonment. In fact, as the Bible tells us, "Perfect love drives out fear."[26]

Virginia Lively told of a vision she once had of Jesus that gives us a glimpse of this kind of love. She wrote: "[The] thing that struck me was his utter lack of con-demnation. I realized at once that he knew me down to my very marrow. He knew all the stupid, cruel, silly things I had ever done. But I also realized that none of these things—nothing I could ever do—would alter the absolute caring, the unconditional love that I saw in his eyes. I could not grasp it! It was too immense a fact. I felt that if I gazed at him for a thousand years, I still could not realize the enormity of that love."[27]

I have no idea why, but God loves us. He believes in us. He trusts us. He pursues us. When we see that, really *see* that, we can't help but love him back. "We love [him] because he first loved us."[28] This focus keeps faith fresh and free from toxicity.

Falling into the Deadly Snare of Legalism

Jesus never spoke against the prostitutes, thieves, drunkards, or tax collectors (the closest thing to organized crime in Israel at the time) in his preaching. He befriended folks from those crowds. But he was completely at odds with the ministry of the Pharisees. Jesus consistently warned his followers to "beware of," to "be careful" about, and to "watch out" for the teachings and lifestyle of the Pharisees. They were the Eagle Scouts of religion, and their thinking was all out of whack. They were legalists.

It can be difficult to catch the error of legalistic reasoning because it begins with the Word of God—and we all should be open to the Word of God. The problem isn't in the legalist's desire to keep God's laws but in the strategy he or she employs for keeping them. Jesus described it like this: "Instead of giving you God's Law as food and drink by which you can banquet on God, they package it in bundles of rules, loading you down like pack animals."[29] It was the bundle of rules they added to God's rules that made Pharisaic, legalistic thinking dangerous.

To ensure that a specific law of God was obeyed, the Pharisees believed they should make up rules that "fenced" people a step back from breaking the actual command. They thought of these "fence laws" as a first line of defense against disobedience. They reasoned that if a person would have to break the man-made fence laws before breaking one of God's real laws, it would be a deterrent and a protection for people. Noble enough.

But they ended up creating hundreds of fence laws dealing with everything from what one could or couldn't wear or eat to what one could or couldn't do on the Sabbath—and with whom. So whether you wanted to pray, fast, rest, or whatever, there were dozens of rules to follow—legalism ruled.

The problem was, there were too many rules to keep track of, much less follow. It wasn't possible to obey them all unless you devoted yourself completely to rehearsing and obeying them—which meant you had to become a Pharisee. The average, barely literate Jewish person could never hope to keep up with these guys.

So the masses of Israelites did the best they could but were pretty much resigned to the fact that they were hopeless failures. And the Pharisees gloated. They loved being the only really holy ones in Israel.

I know a few words in Spanish. I can say hello or ask where the bathroom is, but that's about it. If I would learn more words, I could communicate better with Spanish-speaking people. The Pharisees saw religious rules as a kind of God-language. And they were the only ones who spoke it. They believed the more rules a person knew, the more he or she would be able to commune with God. They believed their legalistic, man-made rituals, formulas, and rules brought people closer to God. But in reality, what they added actually served to nullify the commands of God.[30]

In a world of religious rule keeping—which still exists today—some obey while others do not. The ones who keep the rules feel they've earned the religious Eagle Scout badge, and they wear it with pride. Rule keeping makes you feel like you're on the top perch, where you can look down on others who are less than you—on all us messy spiritual Cub Scouts. And you can't help but feel a responsibility to pressure those of us below you to obey the rules or else be disenfranchised. Some think that's ministry. But it's really classic legalism.

"There is death in the pot!" was the cry of a bunch of prophets-in-training under a powerful Old Testament prophet named Elisha.[31] Someone had innocently thrown some poisonous gourd—perhaps the squirting cucumbers indigenous to that region—into the pot of stew the group was to eat for dinner. I suggest that this is precisely what has happened in the modern-day stew we call Christianity: there is death in the pot. The bad cucumbers are the poisonous rules and ways of legalism.

This is why so many Christians are weak and tired and burned out—too many bad cucumbers in their spiritual diet. This is why many of our teens are quitting church. Jesus is cool—he isn't the problem. We are. We pile rule on top of rule on our kids. We think it's too risky to invite them into a conversation about the reasonableness of God's commands; instead, we shove our musts and shoulds and you-betters down their throats from our never-ending garden of squirting cucumbers.

We can have a safe, nontoxic faith—where the joy, innocence, and purity of faith is untainted. This kind of faith changes everything, and it makes you stand out in some amazing, wonderful ways—like getting answers to prayer and living free from guilt. But it also can get you into trouble. Scripture records that while some folks "conquered kingdoms" and "administered justice" with faith, others "were tortured," "were chained and put in prison," "were stoned," and "sawed in two."[32]

As a small dog, you don't know whether living your faith will lead to conquering kingdoms or being stoned. But you can be assured that such a life *will* have an impact on the world. You may be only one small barking dog, but when you "bark" faith, you live a life that cannot be ignored.

PART THREE

- - - - - - -

Roaming with the Big Dogs

BIG DOGS RULE. EVERY TIME Frank encounters a big dog, he gives way—his ears go down, and he cowers a bit. It's the natural thing to do.

Big humans rule too. And when we run into "big" people, folks with big talent or big personality or big positions, most of us give way—our voices go down, and we cower a bit. It's the natural thing to do.

Let's face it: the world is rigged against small dogs. Everywhere you look, big is rewarded with a higher status and small is shoved aside. A little dog stands out in the world not because he pretends to be big but because he takes seriously the truth that God uses small dogs in a big way.

There are a number of things a small dog can do to safely roam in the big dog world. We look at those next.

Chapter 7

Avoiding the Dread

FRANK'S LIFE IS SINGULARLY LACKING in glamour. The word *routine* comes to mind. Frank is a creature of habit. If you knew Frank well, you would say he leads a fairly repetitive and boring life. But here's the thing: he gives every indication of being perfectly content. One has to wonder if dogs lack the intelligence to hate their routine lives.

Or, think about it another way: Who's really the smart one in this regard? How is it that so many of us humans have come to hate our lives?

An ancient Jewish text captures how life can become a thing of dread. Tell me if this comes close to describing a day you spent at work (or at home) in the past few weeks: "In the morning you will say, 'If only it were evening!' and in the evening, 'If only it were morning!'"[1]

I don't think any of us wants to live in the state of discontent known as dread, along with the stress it creates. So why do we? And what is it about Frank's life (and the life of every other creature on this planet, save we humans) that keeps him on such an even keel? I'm not saying Frank never gets moody—he does. When each of our kids left for college, Frank moped around for days, barely leaving his kennel. (So did my wife and I.)

Still, in his sadness Frank stood tall (at least as tall as a small dog can). He had no crying jag, no emotional meltdown, no calls to a therapist. I didn't notice an eating binge, a television binge, or a stretch of heavy drinking. Generally speaking, the animals appear to have better mental health than we humans do. But why?

Frank loves his life. He doesn't dread Mondays, and he doesn't live for the weekend. In his world, every day is a new opportunity, something to look forward to, and a new day to experience happiness, contentment, and joy. Frank has mastered these things in a way I hope to learn.

Lesson from a Bird

One reason we are stressed out is because we forget to trust God. But we should trust him: he's infinitely more powerful and trustworthy than we are. Humans don't have any control over the most important things: we had nothing to say about when we would be born or whether we would be male or female; if the earth were just a few miles closer to the sun, we would boil to death—a few miles farther away, and we would freeze to death; if there were even a slight change in the oxygen or nitrogen amounts in the air, we'd keel over; and so on. Lots of stuff—critical stuff—is completely beyond our control. Yet we go about bustling to and fro as if our existence depended completely upon us. The psalmist warned long ago, "Man is a mere phantom as he goes to and fro: He bustles about, but only in vain."[2] Such effort is silly.

In trying to help folks see that God the Father is really responsible for human life, Jesus gave his followers the bird's-eye view: "Look at the birds of the air; they do not sow or reap or store away in barns, and yet your heavenly Father feeds them. Are you not much more valuable than they?"[3] He was trying to get his apprentices to trust . . . to chill out a bit . . . to understand that faith in God eliminates much of the needless stress people carry about in life. As the old hymn puts it, "O what needless pain we bear, all because we do not carry everything to God in prayer."

Catherine Marshall, author and wife of well-known minister Peter Marshall, wrote: "If we are to believe in Jesus, His Father and our Father is the God of all life and His caring and provision include a sheepherder's lost lamb, a falling sparrow, a sick child, the hunger pangs of a crowd of four thousand, the need for wine at a wedding feast, and the plight of professional fishermen who toiled all night and caught nothing. These vignettes, scattered through the Gospels like little patches of gold dust, say to us, 'No creaturely need is outside the scope or range of prayer.'"[4]

I've never caught Frank worrying about the future. He just trusts that things will work out. He lives in the present. In fact, what I see in him is reminiscent of Jesus' words: "Do not worry about tomorrow, for tomorrow will worry about itself. Each day has enough trouble of its own."[5] Way to go, Frank. You're a Bible dog.

I, on the other hand, need help here.

I think we humans try to carry weights we were not designed to bear. Too often we carry weights of the future, the past, and actions of other people—things beyond our control. I'm not suggesting that we don't have a role to play in how life turns out—we do.

I'm just saying I don't know if it's as much of a role as we sometimes think it is. And when we try to carry something we can't control, we stress out and become dread pirates.

It seems to me that the most difficult part of Christianity is the whole trust issue. We are called to trust Jesus Christ, not just for salvation, but also for our daily lives. But trust means we have to be comfortable with leaving control of things that directly impact our lives in the hands of someone else. If you have never had a good trust experience—where someone proved trustworthy—you will have a hard time with this. For many, trust has only ever been followed by disappointment.

It is terrifying to think that we don't have the stuff to make it on our own. Something in us wants to believe that if we just really try, we can somehow change the blunt reality that we live in an imperfect and sometimes evil world. Instead of trusting in Another, we would rather trust that if we try harder, life will get better and won't be so bad. We want to believe that bad things can be corrected and that we are the ones who can do something about them.

Trust, on the other hand, means admitting that we don't have what it takes to make it on our own and that we need help. This position feels deeply unsettling. It's like falling backward: instinctively we scramble for control. Something in us fights to prove that we can control our lives.

Quiet terror rises within us when we think we cannot control the ultimate outcome of our lives. So we foster the illusion that life spins out of control for weak people, for those without knowledge or for those who give in too quickly. And we create an illusion of control with our busyness instead of a lifestyle of trust in the person of God.

Here is a simple analogy that may help juxtapose our role with the role God will play as we trust in him: I just turned on the light switch in my family room. I didn't really think about the light switch and how important it was for me to walk up to the wall and throw that switch—I flipped the switch almost unconsciously in response to my need for light. My focus was on getting light into the room. I know that turning the switch on was critical in the process of getting the light I needed, but turning on the switch didn't really create the light, nor did it earn the light. I have no ability within myself to light anything. I need something outside myself to light my world. The flipping of switches is just my way of receiving help—it's a form of trust.

King David wrote a song about not taking bigger bites out of life than we are designed to chew—it's a song-prayer that should be a part of each of our devotional lives: "GOD, I'm not trying to rule the roost, I don't want to be king of the mountain. I haven't meddled where I have no business or fantasized grandiose plans. I've kept my feet on the ground; I've cultivated a quiet heart. Like a baby content in its mother's arms, my soul is a baby content."[6]

Taking ourselves too seriously is destructive to the human soul, but so is not taking ourselves seriously enough. I think the balance is found in Jesus' call: "Come to me, all you who are weary and burdened, and I will give you rest. Take my yoke upon you and learn from me, for I am gentle and humble in heart, and you will find rest for your souls. For my yoke is easy and my burden is light."[7] We do have a role to play—we must "come," we must take Christ's "yoke" and learn from him. But those responsibilities, as critical as they may be, are the smallest part of the deal. And the reward? The reward is no more dread.

Eight Little Words

There they were, eight little words staring at me from the page of the New Testament: "Whoever would love life and see good days . . ."[8] I felt a shot of hope go through me as I read them. I wanted to love life and see good days—who wouldn't? This sounded like the road to a low-stress, dread-free, Franklike existence. But how? The apostle Peter revealed the secret in the next few words: " . . . must keep his tongue from evil and his lips from deceitful speech."[9] It turns out that our words dramatically impact the tone of our lives. Talk isn't cheap after all. In fact, our speech can be one of the most costly aspects of our lives.

Though speech can be deceitful and evil in many ways, let's discuss two: the I'd-rather-be's and words of criticism.

I'd Rather Be's

Wanna have a bad day? Just wake up and say, "I wish I could have slept longer." Then look over at your spouse and think, *I'd rather be married to someone else*. Get in your car and tell yourself, "If only I had a better car." Get to your job and tell someone, "I hate this job. I'd rather work anywhere but here." The I'd-rather-be's are all about focusing on what you'd *rather* have, which fosters disdain for what *is*. This stuff fuels discontentment like nobody's business. It is best captured in the text quoted above: "In the morning you will say, 'If only it were evening!' and in the evening, 'If only it were morning!'"[10] Consummate dread.

This surprises many, but happiness and contentment have little to do with circumstances. They have much more to do with a person's way of thinking. Philosophers and spiritual leaders throughout history have echoed one basic credo: do the best you can; enjoy the present; and rest satisfied with what you have. This, they say, is the root of contentment.

Paul put it this way: "I have learned, in whatsoever state I am, therewith to be content."[11] The ancient philosopher Epictetus wrote: "He is a wise man who does not grieve for the things which he has not, but rejoices for those which he has." The Hebrews writer penned, "Be content with what you have."[12]

We hit a whole new low for the soul when we believe that contentment is somehow contingent on getting more things. Christ-followers have never bought into the idea that life is enhanced when we become the gatherers of more stuff. In fact, in a general sense, stuff-gathering is a waste of precious time and is contrary to our core mission here on planet Earth.

We agree with the witness of the Bible guys and gals—people like . . .

Solomon. Although he admitted, "I denied myself nothing my eyes desired; I refused my heart no pleasure," yet in the end he asserted: "Everything was meaningless, a chasing after the wind; nothing was gained under the sun."[13]

Abraham and Sarah. Although they never seemed to strive to gather wealth, they were actually extremely wealthy (and God was the one who rightly claimed credit for that). Instead of building large houses or enormous mansions (like those they were probably familiar with from Egypt and Babylon), they chose to live simply—wandering around and residing in tents—presumably nice ones, but they were still tents. Scripture says they did this on purpose because they realized "that they were aliens and strangers on earth."[14]

Now there's a radical idea: Abraham and Sarah saw the earth as foreign soil. They didn't think anything here was worth committing their lives to. "Instead," the Bible continues, "they were longing for a better country—a heavenly one. Therefore God is not ashamed to be called their God, for he has prepared a city for them."[15]

David. He asked God to keep him safe from people who loved this world too much: "O LORD, by your hand save me from such men, from men of this world whose reward is in this life."[16]

The apostle John. He warned, "Don't love the world's goods. Love of the world squeezes out love for the Father. Practically everything that goes on in the world—wanting your own way, wanting everything for yourself, wanting to appear important—has nothing to do with the Father. It just isolates you from him. The world and all its wanting, wanting, wanting is on the way out—but whoever does what God wants is set for eternity."[17]

Moses. Here was a guy with it all. He was on the ruling court at the hippest place on earth—this was the LA of the ancient world—glorious Egypt. And Moses was a celebrity. But he chucked it all. The Scriptures say: "By faith, Moses, when grown, refused the privileges of the Egyptian royal house. He chose a hard life with God's people rather than an opportunistic soft life of sin with the oppressors. He valued suffering in the Messiah's camp far greater than Egyptian wealth because he was looking ahead, anticipating the payoff. By an act of faith, he turned his heel on Egypt, indifferent to the king's rage. He had his eye on the One no eye can see, and kept right on going."[18]

Jesus. He said he "did not come to be served, but to serve, and to give his life as a ransom for many."[19] He had an "other" orientation, not a selfish, I'm-here-to-grab-all-the-marbles-I-can orientation. Basically, Jesus' position was that a life lived just for gathering is a life wasted.

Nothing is inherently wrong with possessions, and

God does promise to be our provider,[20] but life is more than just nice cars, new houses, and big boats. Pope John Paul II said: "It is not wrong to want to live better; what is wrong is a style of life which is presumed to be better when it is directed toward 'having' rather than 'being' and which wants to have more not in order to be more, but in order to spend life in enjoyment as an end in itself."[21]

Here's the deal: you and I will never be content, nor will we have good days, if we believe happiness comes from having more stuff or being somewhere else with someone else doing something else. It just won't work. The I'd-rather-be's keep you in the land of dread.

David Grayson wrote, "Contentment, and indeed usefulness, comes as the infallible result of great acceptances, great humilities—of not trying to make ourselves this or that (to conform to some dramatized version of ourselves), but of surrendering ourselves to the fullness of life—of letting life flow through us."[22]

A Critical Spirit

Then there's the business of criticism. If you don't mind missing out on loving life and seeing good days, just embrace the evil tongue and deceitful speech of a critical spirit. Criticism guarantees that contentment won't have a chance in your soul. The critical person judges everything and everyone and finds them wanting.

A critical spirit always pushes, always seeks a fight. Criticism has not a whiff of grace about it. It refuses to be silent and to let things settle and shift, or give people space to reflect and make changes for themselves. No way. A critical spirit is too egocentric to think of others. It focuses on what needs to change and forces the issue. The problem is that too much force gives rise to conflict and argument. Then the relational climate gets hostile. Relationships often require a light touch, but criticism is far too selfish to take anything lightly; it always has a sense of 911 urgency.

Critical people feel justified taking control of situations and people. After all, they are right. The problem is, their "right" is nothing more than an imposed morality (or perspective) that rests entirely on what the critical person perceives should or shouldn't be. Critical people are both calculating and manipulative, assuming the roles of judge and jury, meting out the punishment they see fit for whatever they deem bad behavior.

Criticism may bring some short-term benefit, but when we control people through criticism, they feel violated. Over time they become less open and more defensive. They may do what you think they ought to do, but they cringe inside and may begin to plot revenge. Victories over others through criticism really end in failure.

Just think of how you feel when you're around critical people and feel the backhand of their criticism. Though there may be truth in what they say, there's a residual sting in your soul after hearing their words. The human soul longs for affirmation and encouragement. And as much as we thirst for approval, we dread criticism and condemnation.

I read of a man who received a criticism he carried with him for years. He said when he read of the death of the one who had delivered the blow, he couldn't help but remember the hurt that had been done by him. "If you and I want to stir up a resentment tomorrow that may rankle across the decades and endure until death," he wrote, "just let us indulge in a little stinging criticism—no matter how certain we are that it is justified."[23]

Criticism is deadly to relationships and often boomerangs. It has a monstrous quality about it. And it effectively blocks things like love, goodwill, and mercy. Confronting injustice biblically (which we'll discuss below) is very different from being critical.

Jesus said, "Don't pick on people, jump on their failures, criticize their faults—unless, of course, you want the same treatment. That critical spirit has a way of boomeranging. It's easy to see a smudge on your neighbor's face and be oblivious to the ugly sneer on your own. Do you have the nerve to say, 'Let me wash your face for you,' when your own face is distorted by contempt? It's this whole traveling road-show mentality all over again, playing a holier-than-thou part instead of just living your part. Wipe that ugly sneer off your own face, and you might be fit to offer a washcloth to your neighbor."[24]

Instead of condemning people, we need to try to understand them—to figure out why they do what they do. That ends up being so much more interesting than criticizing, and it breeds a tolerance and kindness that is Christlike.

Let's remember that even God will wait until after our lives are over to judge us. Why do we think we should attempt to judge others now? Anyone can criticize and condemn. It takes a person of real character to dare to work on understanding and forgiving others. Even if you believe your perspective is great and that you outshine most people, that does not give you the right to criticize them. Thomas Carlyle wrote, "A great man shows his greatness by the way he treats little men."

Healthy Criticism?

Almost from the cradle we are taught to be criticizers. Life is a mixture of good and bad—each of our experiences, every relationship, every personality we encounter, every institution has some parts we like and other parts we don't like. Doesn't looking with a critical, analytical eye seem like a good, constructive thing to do, as it helps us locate the things we can improve?

Joyce Maynard wrote of her family:

We could be called opinionated. Certainly we are a hypercritical family—we don't lavish superlatives on things and places and people. I was raised to look closely, not to accept easily. . . . I couldn't suspend judgment even when I wanted to: it was as if I went through life with X-ray glasses on, seeing through not just the things I wanted to see through but the things I'd just as soon have believed in too. . . . The criticism we applied to everything we encountered we applied to ourselves as well. Never "You are bad," but "You could do better." . . . The critical faculties my parents gave me have made me more demanding than I should be, given me standards that the real, flawed world can't live up to."[25]

This kind of critical thinking is generally applauded in our culture. Critical thinking is part of the fabric and spirit of the Renaissance and eighteenth-century rationalism. It encourages us to carefully evaluate people, institutions, and events that surround us. Americans especially belong to a tradition that practically demands that we assess every word spoken and every action taken. And this approach has led to a long history of fighting for change—much of it good. Even the Founders were known as a group who refused to accept unquestioningly the world as it was. They dared to criticize it for its flaws and to imagine a better world.

Over two hundred years has trained us that an uncritical populace is a populace that is indolent and in peril. We believe it is our responsibility to rise up and lift our voices against injustice, poverty, corruption, and the like—even if it means revolt. It is the American way. The whole American Revolution was an example of the kind of "good" that can come out of revolt. Even if a person believes criticism and revolt are wrong on some level, so much good has come out of it, one can't help but wonder if the end justifies the means.

But not everyone agrees. The truth is, when you analyze the steps that lead to divorce, a student shooting spree, a breakout of war, a broken friendship—the process always starts with criticism. Then criticism leads to discontent. The moment discontent gains a foothold, appreciation and gratitude are aborted. Then self-pity grows. We deserve better than what we are experiencing, we reason. So we convince ourselves: This must change. This isn't right. This is completely unacceptable. Over time, as the discontentment and self-pity percolate, we come to the place where we feel justified to do whatever it takes to change the situation—even if our actions end up hurting someone else. After all, we reason, they asked for it in one way or another. If the end we seek brings the happiness and freedom we believe we deserve, it justifies the means by which we get there.

But God says no. He says, "Get rid of all bitterness, rage and anger, brawling and slander, along with every form of malice. Be kind and compassionate to one another, forgiving each other, just as in Christ God forgave you."[26] "Never criticize or condemn—or it will all come back on you."[27]

Christ-followers must renounce criticism.

Paul wrote: "Do everything without complaining or arguing, so that you may become blameless and pure, children of God without fault in a crooked and depraved generation, in which you shine like stars in the universe as you hold out the word of life."[28]

You want to stand out? You want to live large for

God? Then refuse to use criticism as an agent for change.

How to Foster Change without Criticism

We face a host of injustices that scream for reform. But if criticism is forbidden as an agent of change, how do we deal with all the things in this world that need to change? Those of us who are followers of Jesus must find our answer in the actions Jesus took to reform the world. Though his response to evil was never criticism, anger, hatred or violence, he did not sit by idly. His call for change was filtered through three radical methods—methods that we, as his apprentices, must emulate.

Method 1: The Right Motive

Our motive for change must not spring from a Popeye the Sailor moment where we indignantly scream out, "That's all I can stands, and I can't stands no more!" Our motivating force should never be selfish intolerance, hateful revenge, or the prideful "I'm the best and brightest in the room, so you'd better listen to me." Our motivation for change must be a longing for God's interests to be represented, for his kingdom to come. In all our causes and crusades, we need to approach bringing change into the world God's way. We should never be driven by a dismissive or hateful attitude toward people who advocate injustice.

This is hard. Once we witness an injustice, something within us cries out against it and the one who caused it. We feel we must make the perpetrator aware of the pain he or she has caused. The Old Testament laws of God suited our natural impulse to attack the one responsible for injustice. Leviticus instructs: "If anyone injures his neighbor, whatever he has done must be done to him: fracture for fracture, eye for eye, tooth for tooth. As he has injured the other, so he is to be injured."[29]

But then Jesus came and shocked everyone:

You have heard that it was said, "Eye for eye, and tooth for tooth." But I tell you, do not resist an evil person. If someone strikes you on the right cheek, turn to him the other also. And if someone wants to sue you and take your tunic, let him have your cloak as well. If someone forces you to go one mile, go with him two miles. Give to the one who asks you, and do not turn away from the one who wants to borrow from you.

You have heard that it was said, "Love your neighbor and hate your enemy." But I tell you: Love your enemies and pray for those who persecute you, that you may be sons of your Father in heaven.[30]

Jesus introduced the radical idea of not demanding retribution. Somehow Jesus found a way to separate injustice into two issues: (a) the injustice itself and (b) its instigators. Before we deal with any injustice that needs to be remedied, Jesus commands us to love rather than criticize and retaliate against the ones responsible. We are to forgive the perpetrators instead of demanding repayment in kind as the Old Testament allowed. Jesus actually told his followers to be kind to those who have ripped us off emotionally, socially, or physically!

But why? How can he ask us to do that? Who will take the blame and bear the responsibility for wrong actions, if not the person who did the wrong? Where is the justice in that? Where is the truth? Isn't this setting us up for repeated abuse? Isn't Jesus ignoring the need for justice? How is it possible to separate an injustice from the one who doles it out?

To understand why Jesus calls us to respond in this

way, we need to look at the cross. On the cross Jesus became the substitute for all villains. He paid the penalty
for all human sin and injustice. "God made him [Jesus]
who had no sin to be sin for us, so that in him we might
become the righteousness of God."[31]

Injustice is still at play in our world as a result of the
sin of humankind. But God's position is that before injustice can be dealt with directly, the unjust must be
separated from the injustice—and they must be forgiven.

God's deathblow to injustice is through the cross—
through the principle of substitution. As our substitute,
Jesus took the blame and the responsibility for the sin
and injustice of the whole world. That means that God
begins to right injustice and destroy evil by first sepa-
rating every perpetrator, every guilty person, every
enemy to justice from the injustice.

On the cross Jesus opened the door for injustice to
be dealt with in a new way—a way that does not assign
blame to the ones causing the injustice. We no longer
have to "resist an evil person" to establish justice and
bring needed change. As believers, we must (by faith)
see Jesus becoming the guilty party in substitution for
all those who have brought injustice into the world (including us). If we want to fight for change, we must
choose to release (forgive) the person who brought the

offense first. This is how the Christian enters the process of overcoming evil and destroying injustice.

Method 2: Love and Hate the Right Things

Christians are to love the perpetrator of injustice while continuing to hate and make plans to correct the injustice. But something inside us cringes at the idea of loving evil people. We don't want to love them; we want to get even with them. But God's way does not allow this. Nor does it leave room for anger, criticism, defending of our rights, clamming up, or writing people off. We must let go of the part of us that does not want to accept that Jesus has done enough for us to forgive the malevolent offenders.

To effectively deal with injustice, you must pass the love test: you must "Love your enemies and pray for those who persecute you."[32] We must make a clear distinction between the injustice we hate and the person responsible for its occurrence. But this takes a miracle. It's the miracle of the cross, a miracle of substitution (Jesus taking the blame for the person who is guilty). This distinction, this separation of the offense and the offender, opens the way for us to be reconciled to one another, and it must be embraced before we try to quash the evil of injustice.

Now, every time people offend, attack, or otherwise fail us, we don't have to retaliate against them for the demands of justice to be met. Nor do we have to "crucify" our offenders. We must hear Jesus crying from the cross, "Blame me and release (forgive) them from their sin!" Then—and only then—can we deal effectively with injustice.

Method 3: Do What's Right

When we stumble upon (or get ambushed by) injustice, our first response must be to make sure our motive is change for the furtherance of God's kingdom, not for the defense of what we think is right or wrong. Next we must choose to forgive the perpetrator. And only when we have done those things should we act.

Then we must do what's right. When we don't waste energy on wrong motives or on blaming and criticizing people, we can move directly to doing what is right in a given situation. Forget about who's right and who's to blame; make your move to right wrongs and remedy injustice.

But doing what is right is often costly and difficult.

My friend John told me about one of the first jobs he had working for a construction company. The company was fairly large and employed union workers. John worked outside with two other men who had been with the company for years. John was a hard worker, and it started to get him in trouble. The men complained, "Hey, slow down, you're making us look bad!"

John told them he wasn't trying to do that, but he wasn't going to slow down just to make them look better. The tension grew. Those two guys ostracized John. Before long, word spread, and he started getting dismissive looks from everyone.

John had a choice to make. He either had to obey the Scriptures and work as unto the Lord,[33] or he could try to please everyone around him in order to fit in. He decided to try to please God no matter what. But he also knew he couldn't complain about and write off those men for judging him; he had to love and forgive them. For months he ignored their meanness, worked steadily, and looked for every opportunity to make the guys he worked with look better. Eventually he won them over, but it wasn't easy.

Truth is, the story could have ended in the loss of his job, and it wouldn't have been any less of a victory in John's life. The victory is in doing what's right, no matter what it costs you.

God's way to triumph over injustice is through the cross. Humans' way is the way of criticism and rebellion. Traditionally the human race has tried to change the minds of others in two ways: (1) we use physical force to compel others to do what we want, and (2) we use words—we bombard people with persuasive, critical words until they cry uncle. The problem with this kind of victory is that it leaves the hearts and minds of those people untouched and unchanged.

God calls us to something better. He does not call us to vanquish evil using the weapons of evil. Complaining and grumbling are the first rungs on the ladder of rebellion. That's why God calls us to "Do everything without grumbling."[34] Though historically some good has come out of rebellion, the end does not justify the means—at least not for the believer.

A New Rebellion

As believers, we conduct a rebellion of a different sort, in which we dare to die, to suffer, to sacrifice. This is the way of the cross, and it has been transforming the world for more than two thousand years.

Catherine Marshall told the story of a Lutheran pastor she met in Austria. He was a former Nazi storm trooper who had been radically changed by one small barking dog—of pure-blooded Christian pedigree.

In December 1941 the trooper was with the German armies invading Russia. In the Crimea, in heavily wooded terrain, the battle began going against the Germans. As they had to fall back, the German found himself within the Russian lines, separated from his regiment. Alone he made his way through the forest, fearful at every minute of being captured. Suddenly, he saw a thin cloud of smoke coming from the chimney of a hut. Creeping up warily, gun in hand, he knocked on the door. It was answered by a tiny elderly Russian woman.

Shoving past her and searching the hut, he satisfied himself that the woman lived alone. Apparently, her menfolk were off fighting—perhaps had already been killed. To the German's surprise, the woman offered him food and drink. Neither spoke a word of the other's language, but in the end the Russian woman hid the soldier, feeding him and caring for him for three days and nights. The German grew increasingly baffled. Certainly, no worse enemy than he, a Nazi, could have come to the door here in Russia, where Germans murdered more civilians than the total number of Jews killed in all of Europe. The woods swarmed with Russian troops; surely she knew that if she were caught harboring a German she would be shot.

Out of his mounting desire to communicate, he managed through sign language and facial expressions to convey his question, "Why have you risked your life to hide and befriend me?"

The old woman looked at him for a long moment in silence, then turned and pointed to a crucifix on the wall above her bed.

Telling me the incident, the Lutheran pastor added, "After I escaped back to the German lines, try as I would I couldn't forget what happened. I hadn't known love like that was possible. In the end, I was drawn irresistibly to the One who enabled that little Russian lady to prefer another to herself—even when the other was a cruel and deadly enemy. I wanted to know the power of the Cross in my life too. That's why I am a Christian today."[35]

Imagine a world where believers in Christ "bark" at injustice with love-guns blazing; a world where Christ-followers put others ahead of themselves and join a new kind of rebellion—one free from criticism and selfish motives; a world where we let the cross work its change in our hearts.

I think we Christians should long for a better world. We should stand against injustice but in a way that says no to the I'd-rather-be's and to a critical spirit. But our *no* is not an end in itself. It implies a *yes* to something more. We say yes to introducing love and justice where it is missing in the world. We refuse to be selfish, because our lives are grounded in values bigger than our solitary needs, wants, desires, and exaggerated sense of fairness and justice. We seek to advance the kingdom of God.

If we embrace these ideas, we will stand out in a way that cannot be ignored—this dog will hunt! Embracing contentment and refusing to live a life filled with the dread a critical spirit fosters is how ordinary people become extraordinary.

Chapter 8

■■ ■■ ■ ■ ■

Doggie Vision

D OGS CATCH THINGS PEOPLE MISS. Before we ever hear a car rolling up the driveway, Frank is on all fours, ears piqued, with growl starting to rumble. Picking up on nuances that point to coming changes is the stuff of vision. Vision sees beyond the obvious. It picks up on the things others miss; it connects the nuts and bolts of what's going on now to the future.

Small-Dog Vision to Touch the Future

Vision always touches the future, but it does so in two ways: it is either associative, observing the future that is on its way based on what is happening now, or it is predictive, able to see a future that could happen if certain changes occur. Everything that is visible only exists because someone had the vision to get it here. Someone had to imagine it, dream it, and think it before it could materialize—a house, a lifelong achievement, a child well raised, a cure for a disease, a life well lived—it's all the stuff of vision.

Connecting the Dots—Associative Vision

Associative vision points you to the future by giving you intuition about where you're headed based on what's happening right now. If you will dare to take time to imagine what your life will be like in the next five or ten years should you continue down the same path you're on now—that's vision. People's lives end up where they do because people are the way they are. Shakespeare wrote, "The fault . . . is not in our stars, but in ourselves."[1]

Most people don't take the time to really examine their lives, yet they act surprised at what life hands them. That's silly. The ancient philosopher Socrates said, "The unexamined life is not worth living." In other words, happiness is an inside job. You start down the road to happiness when you dare to examine where it is your habits are taking you.

The Scriptures speak loudly to this point. Once Moses told the whole nation of Israel, "This day I call heaven and earth as witnesses against you that I have set before you life and death, blessings and curses. Now choose life, so that you and your children may live."[2] He was telling them they had a choice about the future because they had a choice about how they were going to act in the present. No external force solely determines your future. Connecting the dots between today's actions and how they will lead you to tomorrow's life is what associative vision is all about.

Paul said it this way: "Don't be misled: No one makes a fool of God. What a person plants, he will harvest. The person who plants selfishness, ignoring the needs of others—ignoring God!—harvests a crop of weeds. All he'll have to show for his life is weeds! But the one who plants in response to God, letting God's Spirit do the growth work in him, harvests a crop of real life, eternal life."[3]

If you will take the time to do a life checkup right now, you'll be able to predict where you're headed, as surely as smoke leads to fire. It's a simple-addition equation, like $2 + 2 = 4$.

- Going out every night and getting drunk + ten years = alcoholism.

- Spending more than you earn + borrowing more and more money to keep up with your runaway spending habits = bankruptcy.

- Treating your spouse like he or she is an inconvenience + avoiding communication = divorce.

This isn't rocket science. Vision lets you see what's coming. It connects the dots from what is to what will be—unless you change something.

Telling the Future—Predictive Vision

The good news about vision is that it not only helps you see what will happen in the future based on current data, but it will help you imagine a different future and have the wisdom to know what to do to move toward that future. It works both ways.

That means that if you examine your life and if you don't like the future that's coming, you can change it! Your career, your relationships, your faith, your physical health—all are subject to change. And the equation is still the simple $2 + 2 = 4$.

- Ceasing to stuff your face with everything you see + walking two or three times a week = a healthy, more energetic life.

- Going back to college + working hard on the agonizing papers and tests = hopeful new career opportunities.

- Daring to put your spouse before your work + giving him or her scads of undivided attention = a revitalized, happy marriage.

Go ahead and ask yourself what needs to be changed. Then decide what to do to change it and when you'll start. Dare to have the vision to see where it is you are currently heading, and then dare to imagine a different life—one that is better than what you have accomplished thus far. The bottom line is that we create many of our own opportunities in life when we take responsibility for our lives.

Lost Imagination

Albert Einstein said, "Imagination is more important than knowledge."[4] Unfortunately, imagination is one of the first things lost in our American education system. Though many heroic teachers abhor it, conformity (the anti-imagination) rules at school. Remember the tree you had to draw in kindergarten? If you were imaginative and drew something a bit aesthetic or emotive, your teacher probably corrected you and showed you how to draw a tree. That's when the death of vision began. Conformity kills vision because imagination is the core competency needed to be a visionary person. Most of us had our imaginations completely quashed by the third grade. You just don't get rewarded for originality in grade school (or high school for that matter)—you get A's for imitating. The aim is for conformity and standardization.

By the time most of us hit adulthood, creativity and ingenuity are things of the past. Psychiatrist Rollo May wrote: "The clearest picture of the empty life is the suburban man, who gets up at the same hour every weekday morning, takes the same train to work in the city, performs the same task at the office, lunches at the same place, leaves the same tip for the waitress each day, comes home on the same train each night, and has 2.3

children, goes to church every Christmas and Easter, and moves through a routine mechanical existence year after year until he finally retires at sixty-five and very soon thereafter dies of heart failure. . . . I've always had the secret suspicion, however, that he dies of boredom."[5]

Somewhere along the road we lose the art of letting our minds wander off and imagine what can be versus what is. The imagination police in school and the workplace keep us from venturing off the familiar trails into the world of the unexplored—yet only there is originality found. Originality is the fruit of vision and exploration—you must be willing to go out into unexplored territory. And you're going to need a backpack and some good walking boots to get there—there are no marked paths or roads.

Vision is intelligence having fun—it's fun to imagine not just what is but what can be. Vision sees what everyone else sees but dares to think about it differently. It pays attention to where things are going and understands the nuts and bolts behind it. But it also sees which nuts and bolts can be adjusted to change the future. Vision requires the curiosity of a child and the observation skills of a scientist. Visionaries adjust the future by fidgeting with the present. Being a visionary helps you see the possibilities of tomorrow within the realities of today. It helps you dig a well before you get thirsty.

Perhaps the two greatest gifts vision gives are seeing beneath the surface to the heart of an issue and problem solving.

Seeing Beneath the Surface

Often what changes the world is this: taking what is already known and applying that knowledge in a way no one has thought of applying it before. Ideas that change everything are often just beneath our feet, right under our noses, before our very eyes, or on the tips of our tongues.

History is full of important medical and scientific breakthroughs that happened almost accidently—when someone was willing to look at the world differently and make a connection that hadn't been made before. Those people had vision.

Laminated glass was invented in 1903 by French chemist Edouard Benedictus. During an experiment, he accidentally dislodged a glass flask that had contained cellulose nitrate, a liquid plastic. When it fell to the floor with the expected crash, the flask shattered. But Benedictus was surprised that the pieces didn't scatter; they held together, and the bottle kept its shape. Upon further examination he discovered that there had been a solvent in the flask that had evaporated, leaving a thin, invisible skin on the walls of the bottle that kept it together though the glass had shattered. Shortly after this, Benedictus was reading a newspaper article about a girl who had been in a car accident and was seriously cut by flying glass. He made the connection between the two incidents in his mind and invented laminated safety glass.

Problem Solving

The real power of vision is that it gives you the ability to make some complicated problems amazingly simple—which leads to solutions. Vision helps you clearly see the future your current steps are taking you to. Then it gives you the ability to imagine a different future and helps you know the right step to take first . . . leading to the next right step . . . which leads you inexorably to the new vision you've imagined. Problem solved.

J. R. R. Tolkien wrote, "All that is gold does not glitter; not all those that wander are lost."[6] When you bump into a problem, don't be afraid to wander a bit in your imagination. When you wander off the established trail, you just may stumble onto something well worth thinking about. One idea can lead to another, and you may find yourself with a whole new arsenal of solutions.

The God of Visions and Dreams

I think people of faith should be ahead of the curve when it comes to having vision. Why? Because visions and dreams are God's domain. In Acts 2 we see the beginning fulfillment of God's promise to pour out his Spirit into the world, leading people to "see visions" and "dream dreams."[7] God's Spirit can't help but fuel our dreams and vision. Vision is a kind of language of the Holy Spirit. God did not create us to be specialized drones that just do what they're designed to do. We think. We see relationships and possibilities and put them together in surprising new ways. We are more than the sum of our parts, and our minds are able to take creative leaps beyond present boundaries. And why not? We are in relationship with the Creator, so it's only natural that we can create, as he does—at least a little.

We create music and art. We see problems and, as we think them through, we create solutions. We see needs and create inventions to meet those needs. Our desires (whether good or bad) cause us to creatively

cook up ways to secure what we desire. We find path-
ways to get us to what we love. This is one of the ways
we reflect God's image—we are minicreators. And this
is why all human beings can have hope: whether we are
saints or sinners, we all have the power to change our
lives.

Being people of vision is big part of what makes humans so different from the rest of the animal kingdom.
We can imagine being just about anything we want to
be. Perhaps we should do so more often than we do.
Robert A. Heinlein wrote, "A human being should be
able to change a diaper, plan an invasion, butcher a hog,
conn a ship, design a building, write a sonnet, balance
accounts, build a wall, set a bone, comfort the dying,
take orders, give orders, cooperate, act alone, solve
equations, analyze a new problem, pitch manure, program a computer, cook a tasty meal, fight efficiently, die
gallantly. Specialization is for insects."[8]

We—especially people of faith—should find new
ways to do things and new things to do. Proverbs says
God will give us wisdom for "witty inventions."[9] Being
submissive and obedient to the Creator should not lead
us to indolence and conventionality because we're
shocked and awed by sovereignty. We are not supposed
to become brain-dead automatons. I completely dis-
agree with Karl Marx's assessment that "Religion is the

opium of the people." Opiates drain people, rob them of their creative capacities, and make them settle for whatever is. True religion is more like LSD or cocaine—the imaginative and good-vibe energy drugs (I'm not condoning drug use . . . just sticking with the metaphor—probably for too long).

The Book of Imagination

Scripture records God's commanding believers, "Forget the former things; do not dwell on the past. See, I am doing a new thing! Now it springs up; do you not perceive it?"[10] God has always wanted his people to "perceive" or envision what he was about to do—that's vision. In fact, all the promises of God come across as invitations to have vision.

Think of what could happen if we saw all the promises of God as invitations to imagine what could be? What if God gave these promises to us to help us imagine a better world, a world that "will be filled with the knowledge of the glory of the LORD, as the waters cover the sea"?[11] What if we were to imagine a world where the church is salt and light,[12] where we make life a little more palatable for people and dispel darkness?

What if we were to embrace a vision of a world where . . .

- believers fearlessly contend with evil and make no peace with oppression;

- the church consistently uses its freedom to maintain justice in our communities and among the nations;

- believers imagine themselves to be (as our Savior, Jesus, was) those who come not to be served but to serve;

- by following in Jesus' steps, we have the wisdom, patience, and courage to minister in his name to the suffering, the friendless, and the needy.

Imagine that.

What if prayer itself is a visionary act? Maybe we are supposed to imagine an answer when we come to God in prayer. Jesus said, "Whatever you ask for in prayer, believe that you have received it, and it will be yours."[13] Maybe Jesus was daring us to actually believe when we pray that what we pray for is ours—to literally imagine it!

This would mean we could ask God to help us

imagine world peace. Through prayer we could imagine a world free from hunger and prejudice; a world where we see the fulfillment of God's promise to pour out his Spirit on all people. Imagine the nations coming to God in worldwide spiritual renewal and the fulfillment of the promise, "Ask of me, and I will make the nations your inheritance, the ends of the earth your possession."[14] What if we asked and actually imagined an answer?

What if Paul wasn't kidding when he spoke of God as being "able to do immeasurably more than all we ask or *imagine*"?[15] What if we dared imagine more? What if we took the thoughts of God—his promises and hope for the world—into our minds (vis-à-vis the Scriptures) and opened up our souls for the Holy Spirit to impart God's fruit into us—love, joy, peace, patience, kindness, goodness, faithfulness, gentleness, and self-control?[16] Imagine that!

What if God gave us biblical prophecy not so we could hold the daily news in one hand and the Bible in the other—carefully reading the *New York Times* and the *Jerusalem Post* the way a psychic reads tea leaves to find timelines for the fulfillment of Bible prophecy—but to give us a snapshot of the future he intends to give his people? What if he wants us to have that snapshot so we can cultivate a vision of what the future is going to be—of what the world is going to be like?

The Bible promises that a day is coming when "the dwelling of God" will be with people, "and he will live with them." It says that we "will be his people," and God himself will be with us and be our God. And then it promises: "He will wipe every tear from their eyes. There will be no more death or mourning or crying or pain, for the old order of things has passed away."[17]

Imagine with me a world where God always dwells with us and where all tears are wiped away and all weeping and sorrow are gone. What if we are to carry that vision in our minds?

Theologians tell us that there is an "eschatological tension" in the kingdom of God—that in one sense the kingdom of God is here, but in another sense not yet. Jesus said, "The kingdom of God is at hand";[18] yet he spoke of it as coming in the future. It's on a continuum somewhere between now and not yet. And apparently believers have something to do with where it is. Jesus told us to pray to the Father, asking, "thy kingdom come, thy will be done in earth, as it is in heaven."[19]

However much of the kingdom we can experience here, we know we will never fully have it until Jesus returns. But the kingdom is among us in some measure, and it can be experienced here now—at least like the measles: in spots. What if we exercised vision to see it grow in our lives and in this world?

If we thought this way, when we encountered the tears and laments and suffering so present in this fallen world, we would move toward it, bringing with us the hope of that eternal vision. Maybe that's what ministry is supposed to be.

Perhaps this is what the writer of Hebrews was referring to when he wrote that followers of Jesus could partake of "the powers of the coming age."[20] It is with these thoughts in mind that the *Book of Common Prayer* leads us to pray, "Give to us the peace and unity of that heavenly City."[21]

The Bible is clear that the promises of God don't just happen. We are not to sit back and wait for God to change the world. Hebrews' author admonished, "We do not want you to become lazy, but to imitate those who through faith and patience inherit what has been promised."[22]

I'm suggesting that those of us in the church need to use the power of vision for the glory of God and the advancement of his kingdom. There's more! That's what vision promises us.

There's More

In J. R. R. Tolkien's classic *The Hobbit*, Bilbo Baggins lived contentedly in his home at Bag End, on Hobbiton Hill, until one morning the wizard Gandalf visited him. Gandalf, sensing a hunger for adventure beating secretly in Bilbo's heart, said to him, "There is more in you."

Bilbo, it turns out, was part of the Took clan on his mother's side. The Tooks had been noble defenders of the Shire for centuries and had a reputation for being rather more adventuresome than the typical Hobbit. Gandalf knew that although Bilbo may have inherited the easygoing nature of the Bagginses, his Tookish thirst for adventure would eventually lead him to go beyond the safety of the Shire on a quest that would save Middle-earth.

I believe God put something Tookish in all of us. Erwin McManus wrote: "There was a voice screaming inside my head, Don't sleep through your dreams! Ever heard that voice? It calls you like a temptress to abandon the monotony of life and to begin an adventure. It threatens to leave you in the mundane if you refuse to risk all that you have for all that could be."[23]

Something inside us wants to be part of saving the world. True, we have those things we inherited from

Adam that make us cower and slip into survival and protection mode, but we also have a drive in us that wants to make a difference—that wants to glorify God. We don't have to settle for a life as bean-counting legalists who only color between the lines—we can be spiritual pioneers, adventurers who dare to explore what a life fully committed to God can really look like. We want vision.

I want my days to matter. I don't want to be guilty of the sin of sloth. *Sloth* is defined as "the lack of desire to perform work or expend effort." It's one of the historical seven deadly sins. Sloth, in the context of spiritual life, means not making a priority what we should, or not seeking to change what we should in ourselves. We become apathetic, which means we have no feeling or motivation to act. This sin was present in Israel when Jesus lamented over the city of Jerusalem: "O Jerusalem, Jerusalem, you who kill the prophets and stone those sent to you, how often I have longed to gather your children together, as a hen gathers her chicks under her wings, but you were not willing! Look, your house is left to you desolate."[24]

For Christians, spiritual sloth sometimes means we really don't participate in challenging spiritual vision, experiences, or events. It's easier to spend our time glutting our souls with TV dramas and comedies. It's a lot more work to imagine a different world and to engage with people or ideas that call us to action: to loving our neighbor, helping the poor, or telling the truth when it's not popular.

Being a disciple, or apprentice, of Jesus suggests you are going beyond just believing in the message of redemption and experiencing personal forgiveness—that's certainly where it begins, but that's not where it ends. Following Jesus is an adventure in being counter-cultural. It's embarking on a mission to change the world. This goes beyond simply dedicating one's life to faithful service to build up a local church congregation—its programs, numbers, and facilities. This is about a change of heart, about imagining what life could be like if we put more of our skin in the game to bring God's justice to an unjust world.

The first step to doing something is imagining it—having a vision for it. This is the language of the Holy Spirit. Don't let life stomp this out of you! Never let the facts get in the way of your imagination. What *is* cannot trump what *can be*.

When they look at life this way, even the smallest of dogs can live large.

Epilogue

I F BEING A WORLD CHANGER were limited to those with superior intellect, surpassing talent, and stellar connections in the halls of power, the world wouldn't get changed very much. Only a small handful of humans qualify as great, while the vast majority of us rise to the level of fairly ordinary. But changing the world isn't just for the big dogs—it is possible for anyone. We start down the trail of living a life that matters by realizing we are not accidents but on-purpose creations by God, and by living our lives well.

You may be ordinary and smallish, but that's okay—you can still live in a way that can't be ignored. And what's sweet is, you won't have to pretend to be anything other than who you are in the process. Understanding this will give you the courage to fully be yourself along with the sheer delight of knowing you are destined to be God's agent for change in the world. But the key to actually pulling this off is taking *action*.

Good Works

Changing the world demands engaging in doing *good works*—not works that are oriented to our salvation—those would be "dead works." We are to engage in "good works" because we have been touched and salvaged by God. Paul claimed that when we discover that Jesus "gave himself for us to redeem us from all wickedness and to purify for himself a people that are his very own," we become "eager to do what is good."[1] Living in a way that matters means we push past mere *intention* and into *action*.

In the spring of 2007, a great movie was released based on the true story of William Wilberforce's life, entitled *Amazing Grace*. Wilberforce and a group of friends gathered together at Clapham, South London, in the late 1700s and early 1800s to commit to a common goal of changing the world. This little group, known as the Clapham Sect, consisted of business people, clergymen, politicians, and a playwright. The most famous among them was Wilberforce, who was a member of Parliament.

Wilberforce has an amazing conversion experience at age twenty-six and considered resigning from politics to go into the ministry. It was John Newton (a former slave-trader and author of the hymn "Amazing Grace") who convinced him that God was the one who had put him in Parliament and that he should fight for the abolition of slavery. The group regularly met in the home of a wealthy banker to scheme about changing society and evangelizing the world. They not only fought slavery but worked to improve conditions for workers, established several missionary societies, started schools, worked to ban bullfighting, and secured permission for missionaries to go to India.

But it all came through much work, personal financial cost, and years lived under the threat of assassination by the slave lobby—Wilberforce actually had a nervous breakdown and nearly died. But eventually the Clapham Sect achieved their lifelong dream to emancipate slaves and make them British citizens. A small group of individuals committing to common goals were able to change the whole world. Action changes the world.

The World of Intention

I have a friend who recently told me that a few months ago he and about six other dads were gathered around the TV watching a football game. A conversation erupted about their young boys (each of them has a son around the age of fifteen). My friend said they all got stoked about the idea of doing four major father/son events a year as a group. They even talked about what those events would look like and how they would use their time together to inculcate values and issues of faith into their boys. They left the game that night eager and expectant.

But as the weeks passed, my friend, who was the one responsible to set up the *first* father-son event, found himself putting the trip planning on the back burner—life has a way of "back-burnering" the best intentions. By the time he got back to the other men, about eight weeks had passed. But by then all the emotion of that night had been forgotten, and he could only get *one* of the dads to commit to anything.

Didn't the rest of the dads care? Of course they did. Didn't they love their boys enough to do it? Yes, they did. But here's the problem: we are fooled by *intention*. We judge other people by their actions—what they do or don't do—but we tend to judge ourselves by our *intentions*. I can't tell you how many times my wife has asked me to do something (like clean the garage) and I *intended* to do it. But an unexpected phone call came or a friend stopped by and it didn't happen. I think, *no big deal* because I *intended* to do it.

Gail, on the other hand, only sees that something she has asked me to do goes undone. She doesn't see my intentions, so she's disappointed. Bottom line is that intention really doesn't accomplish *anything*. The garage is still dirty. If something is worth *intending*, it is worth actually *doing*.

Real Vision

Part of the problem is that many of us are used to doing "vision" vicariously. I think we catch it from watching television. The word television literally means seeing something ("vision") from a distance ("tele"). In the West television has become just that—living life "from a distance." Millions stare at their TV screens night after night mesmerized by news shows, dramas, comedies, documentaries, romantic, and action features that broadcast a mixture of the real, the imaginary, and the exaggerated into their homes and lives. These viewers are living, but they are living secondhand, one step removed from the lives they are watching.

I'm a big fan of the series *24*, featuring Kiefer Sutherland as superagent Jack Bauer. *Whoa.* By the time I watch him get shot, stabbed, or tortured, get up and chase a bad guy a few miles on foot, kill three to four people in hand-to-hand combat along the way, catch that bad guy he was chasing, and get him back to CTU for interrogation all in *one* episode . . . I'm exhausted. Though I've been sitting the whole time, I feel like I have worked out, courageously deterred a terrorist from his or her diabolical scheme to hurt the United States, and brought some good old-fashioned justice on several deserving thugs. A busy night indeed. And all done vicariously through my imagined *me*—Jack Bauer—and all from the privacy of my very own living room. It's me living life "from a distance."

Sadly, this is the way many live out the "vision" for their lives—*from a distance*. We want to influence the world—to have our "bark" heard—but we want to do it with minimum involvement. The problem is it won't work. We need to get our "skin" in the game. We need to actually engage in the mission by getting off our blessed assurance and *doing* something—this is the stuff of *real* "vision," not the "tele" kind.

The Order of The Mustard Seed

In his book, *The Vision and the Vow*, Pete Grieg explores the fascinating vow of the eighteenth-century Count Ludwig Nicklaus von Zinzendorf and a few of his friends. The group called themselves the Honourable Order of The Mustard Seed. Each of the members wore a ring with the inscribed motto, "None live for themselves," and they vowed to be true to Christ, to be kind to people, and to take the Gospel of Christ to the nations.[2]

It all began with Zinzendorf and five of his friends in high school. They all had a hand in a revival that swept through their school and felt that God wanted to use them as a team. After they went off in different directions to college, they stayed connected via letter. Then in the spring of 1718, they arranged a meeting where they formally took vows that brought the Order into being. This small group of men, who had vowed to keep each other at the task of being true to Christ, kind to people, and spreading the Gospel, did everything from establishing mission endeavors to spurning significant revivals. They changed the world in which they lived, leaving it better than they found it. This is the power of action.

It is when we *act* that the world is changed and we

become "splendors" for God. The small-dog life is all about *action*. CS Lewis once said, "There are no ordinary people. You have never met a mere mortal. Nations, cultures, arts, civilizations—these are mortal and their life is to ours as a gnat. But it is immortals whom we joke with, work with, marry, snub, and exploit—immortal horrors or everlasting splendors."[3] Our choices determine whether we are "horrors" or "splendors." Which do you want to be?

Decide that your life is going to matter—no matter how big or small you are. Act, speak, and engage using all the persistence, courage, vision, and faith you can muster—master the small-dog life, and you will live a life that's hard to ignore.

Happy barking.

Notes

Chapter 1: Rethink Small

1. Dallas Willard, *The Divine Conspiracy: Rediscovering Our Hidden Life in God* (San Francisco: HarperSan-Francisco 1998), 1.
2. Matthew 23:11.
3. Matthew 20:16.
4. Jimmy Stewart, as told to Richard H. Schneider, "It IS a Wonderful Life," *Guideposts*, October 24, 2008, http://www.guideposts.com/story/Jimmy-Stewart-wonderful-life.
5. *Pulpit Helps*, June 1988.
6. John 1:46.

7. Willard, *Divine Conspiracy*, 14.

8. Romans 11:33.

9. Ruth 1:16.

10. See Acts 13:22.

Chapter 2: Fight the Big-Dog Lie

1. 2 Corinthians 10:12.

2. Ecclesiastes 2:8.

3. Song of Songs 7:4.

4. Song of Songs 4:5.

5. Song of Songs 7:2.

6. Leo F. Buscaglia, *Loving Each Other: The Challenge of Human Relationships* (Thorofare NJ: Slack, 1984), 14.

7. QuoteDB.com,http://www.quotedb.com/quotes/318.

8. Psalm 100:3.

9. Compiled by the Roundtable Association of Diocesan Social Action Directors, National Pastoral Life Center Editorial Board, *Living God's Justice: Reflections and Prayers* (Cincinnati, OH: St. Anthony Messenger Press, 2006), 17.

10. 1 Corinthians 12:22.

11. 1 Corinthians 12:24.

12. 1 Corinthians 12:25.

13. 1 Corinthians 4:7.

14. Matthew 4:8.

15. Deuteronomy 29:29.

16. Acts 26:18.

17. Habakkuk 2:14.

Chapter 3: Dare to Be Small

1. Psalm 139:14.

2. Psalm 115:13.

3. Willard, Dallas, *The Divine Conspiracy: Rediscovering Our Hidden Life In God* (San Francisco: Harper Collins, 1997), 14.

4. See Acts 17:26.

5. Psalm 139:16.

6. See Psalm 139:13.

7. Philippians 4:13 AMP.

Chapter 4: Holding On

1. "Helen Keller Quotes," http://womenshistory.about.com/od/disabilities/a/qu_helen_keller.htm.

2. Lillian Eichler Watson, ed., *Light from Many Lamps* (New York: Simon & Schuster, 1951), 90–91.

3. 1 Corinthians 3:21–22.

4. Galatians 6:7.
5. Matthew 25:24–25.
6. "Persistance," Dennis Bretz, http://www.geocities
   .com/chrestomathy/perseverance.html.
7. Bill Hybels, *Who You Are When No One's Looking: Choosing Consistency, Resisting Compromise* (Downers Grove, IL: InterVarsity, 1987), 52.
8. See 1 Corinthians 10:13.
9. See Romans 12:2.
10. Proverbs 23:7, author paraphrase.
11. 2 Corinthians 4:4 NLT.
12. 2 Peter 1:4.
13. 2 Corinthians 10:4–5 NLT.
14. Philippians 4:8 MSG.
15. http://findquotations.com/quote/by/Calvin_Coolidge

Chapter 5: Courage

1. 2 Timothy 1:7.
2. QuoteDB.com,http://www.quotedb.com/quotes/2437.
3. Watson, *Light from Many Lamps*, 84.
4. Stephen Covey, *Everyday Greatness: Inspiration for a Meaningful Life* (Nashville: Rutledge Hill, 2006), 97.
5. Covey, *Everyday Greatness*, 76.

6. 2 Corinthians 10:4.

7. Peter Scazzero, *Emotionally Healthy Spirituality: Unleash the Power of Authentic Life in Christ* (Nashville: Integrity, 2006), 24.

8. Scazzero, *Emotionally Healthy Spirituality*, 26.

9. Scazzero, *Emotionally Healthy Spirituality*, 53 (adaptation).

10. Hebrews 5:14 NASB.

11. Adapted from Dr. Paul Brand and Philip Yancey, *Pain: The Gift Nobody Wants* (New York: HarperCollins, 1993), 6–7.

12. Luke 23:46.

13. Psalm 90:12.

14. Hebrews 2:15.

15. Philippians 1:20–24 NLT.

16. Charles Hembree, *Pocket of Pebbles* (Grand Rapids: Baker, 1969), 33.

17. William Shakespeare, *Julius Caesar*, act 2, sc. 2.

18. "The Origin of Our Serenity Prayer," AAHistory.com, http://www.aahistory.com/prayer.html.

19. William Norman Grigg, "General George S. Patton—Liberty's Steamroller," *New American*, December 20, 1999, posted on FreeRepublic.com, http://www.freerepublic.com/focus/news/1017644/posts.

Chapter 6: The Bark of Faith

1. Romans 12:2.

2. Romans 12:2.

3. See Genesis 2:7.

4. See Romans 8:20–21.

5. John 3:3.

6. Stephen Crane, *War Is Kind and Other Lines* (Toronto: Dover Publications, 1998), 36.

7. Carl Sagan, *Cosmos* (New York: Random House, 1980), 4.

8. Jean-Paul Sartre, "Nausea" (New York: New Directions Publishers, 1964), 180.

9. Hebrews 13:5–6.

10. Romans 8:31, 37.

11. Philippians 2:15.

12. Exodus 33:15.

13. Matthew 28:19–20.

14. Revelation 2:4.

15. Revelation 2:5.

16. Psalm 63:8 AMP.

17. Exodus 33:15, author paraphrase.

18. 1 Corinthians 6:19.

19. Galatians 2:20.

20. See 1 Corinthians 12.

21. 1 Corinthians 9:22.

22. See Ephesians 2:8.

23. Psalm 139:6 MSG.

24. Ephesians 3:18 NLT.

25. Packard, James I. *Knowing God* (Downer's Grove, IL: Intervarsity Press, 1973), 37.

26. 1 John 4:18.

27. Lively, Virginia, *Healing In His Presence* (Grand Rapids, MI: Zondervan, 1984), 18–19.

28. 1 John 4:19.

29. Matthew 23:4 MSG.

30. See Mark 7:13.

31. 2 Kings 4:40.

32. Hebrews 11:33, 35–37.

Chapter 7: Avoiding the Dread

1. Deuteronomy 28:66–67.

2. Psalm 39:6.

3. Matthew 6:26.

4. Catherine Marshall, *Something More* (New York: McGraw-Hill, 1974), 191.

5. Matthew 6:34.

6. Psalm 131:1–2 MSG.

7. Matthew 11:28–30.

8. 1 Peter 3:10a.

9. 1 Peter 3:10b.

10. Deuteronomy 28:67.
11. Philippians 4:11 KJV.
12. Hebrews 13:5.
13. Ecclesiastes 2:10–11.
14. Hebrews 11:13.
15. Hebrews 11:16.
16. Psalm 17:14.
17. 1 John 2:15–17 MSG.
18. Hebrews 11:24–27 MSG.
19. Matthew 20:28.
20. See Philippians 4:19.
21. The Roundtable Association of Diocesan Social Action Directors, comp., *Living God's Justice: Reflections and Prayers* (Cincinnati: St. Anthony Messenger, 2006), 11.
22. Watson, *Light from Many Lamps*, 10.
23. Dale Carnegie, *How to Win Friends and Influence People* (New York: Pocket Books, 1998), 12–13.
24. Matthew 7:1 MSG.
25. Joyce Maynard, "My Parents Are My Friends," *McCall's*, October 1972.
26. Ephesians 4:31–32.
27. Luke 6:37 TLB.
28. Philippians 2:14–16.
29. Leviticus 24:19–20.
30. Matthew 5:38–45.

31. 2 Corinthians 5:21.

32. Matthew 5:44.

33. See Ephesians 6:5.

34. Phil 2:14 Today's New International Version.

35. Marshall, *Something More*, 229–30.

Chapter 8: Doggie Vision

1. Shakespeare, *Julius Caesar*, act 1, sc. 2.

2. Deuteronomy 30:19.

3. Galatians 6:7–8 MSG.

4. The Quotations Page, http://www.quotationspage .com/quote/703.html.

5. Rollo May, ed., Man's Search for Himself (W. W. Norton & Co: New York, 2009), 9.

6. QuoteDB.com, http://www.quotedb.com/quotes/ 2261.

7. Acts 2:17.

8. Robert A. Heinlein, *Time Enough for Love: The Lives of Lazarus Long* (New York: Ace, 1988), 248.

9. Proverbs 8:12 KJV.

10. Isaiah 43:18–19.

11. Habakkuk 2:14.

12. Matthew 5:13–14.

13. Mark 11:24.

14. Psalm 2:8.

15. Ephesians 3:20, emphasis added.

16. See Galatians 5:22–23.

17. Revelation 21:3–4.

18. Mark 1:15 KJV.

19. Matthew 6:10 KJV.

20. Hebrews 6:5.

21. *Book of Common Prayer* (New York: Oxford University Press, 1990), 138.

22. Hebrews 6:12.

23. Erwin Raphael McManus, *Chasing Daylight* (Nashville: Thomas Nelson, 2002), 5.

24. Luke 13:34–35.

Epilogue

1. John 10:10 MSG.

2. Titus 2:14.

3. Greig, Pete, *The Vision And The Vow, Re-discovering Life and Grace* (Lake Mary, FL: Relevant Books 2004), 131.

4. CS Lewis in *The Weight of Glory*—Commemoration of Charles Williams, 1945.

Acknowledgments

There are so many people who have contributed to this writing—ordinary people who had an extraordinary impact in my life without being aware they were doing so. It was these individuals—men and women, young and old, rich and poor, friends and strangers—who inspired this project.

One of the most notable individuals—an expert in the *small dog way of life*—was my father-in-law, Gerard Arthur Griesbaum. He died the other day just a few days short of his ninetieth birthday. He was not famous or wealthy in the way one normally thinks of such things, but he was a hero to us. His integrity, kindness, and celebration of the ordinary remain legendary. Our hearts will ache in his absence.

Special thanks go to my colleague, Andrew Arndt, who gave me valuable input as he wrestled through that bumpy first draft (he's a patient man). To Roger Bruhn who helped me organize my life in such a way that this book was actually finished while juggling my responsibilities as the lead pastor of Sanctuary in Tulsa, OK (www.sanctuarytulsa.com). And, of course, to the wonderful members and staff of Sanctuary who put up with their pastor disappearing for weeks at a time to noodle and write. They are a bunch of really cool people.

Lastly, I need to give a shout out to the kind Philis Boultinghouse, my brilliant editor and friend, and to Tina Jacobson for her guidance and encouragement.

About the Author

ED GUNGOR is a veteran pastor who became a follower of Christ as a teenager in the early 1970s. He has been deeply involved in the spiritual formation of others for over thirty-five years. Ed has a passion for authentic transformation, a phenomenon he feels is all too rare in today's church.

As a kind of church futurist, he is constantly aware of the changing needs of the next generation of Christians. Ed is known for his down-to-earth and engaging communication style. Gungor enthusiastically cuts through the usual "churchspeak," gleefully slaughtering any sacred cows that distort the true message of Christ. He is the author of several books, including *There Is*

More to the Secret, which landed on the *New York Times* bestseller list. He has also written *What Bothers Me Most about Christianity* and *Religiously Transmitted Diseases.*

Ed and his wife, Gail, have been married thirty years. They have four children and live in Tulsa, Oklahoma. Ed currently serves as lead pastor at Sanctuary Church in Tulsa and travels around the United States and abroad speaking in churches and universities. For more information, visit http://edgungor.com.

Printed in the United States
By Bookmasters